LOOK BEFORE YOU LOVE

LOOK BEFORE YOU LOVE

FENG SHUI TECHNIQUES FOR REVEALING ANYONE'S TRUE NATURE

NANCILEE WYDRA

AUTHOR OF *FENG SHUI: THE BOOK OF CURES*

CONTEMPORARY BOOKS

Library of Congress Cataloging-in-Publication Data

Wydra, Nancilee.
   Look before you love : feng shui techniques for revealing anyone's
true nature / Nancilee Wydra.
       p.   cm.
   Includes bibliographical references and index.
   ISBN 0-8092-2873-4
   1. Feng-shui.   I. Title.
BF1779.F4W94   1998
133.3'337—dc21   98-17925
                                                                      CIP

Interior design by Mary Lockwood
Interior illustrations by Ginny Piech Street

Published by Contemporary Books
A division of NTC/Contemporary Publishing Group, Inc.
4255 West Touhy Avenue, Lincolnwood (Chicago), Illinois 60646-1975 U.S.A.
Printed in the United States of America
International Standard Book Number: 0-8092-2873-4
15   14   13   12   11   10   9   8   7   6   5   4   3   2   1

To my mother, who taught me how to see, and to my father, who taught me how to act, I am grateful for these gifts. Now it is my turn to pass them on to the next generation. To the child of my heart, Zachary, and the children of my spirit, Chloe, Barnaby, Nancy, Shana, Patrick, and Vanessa, I bequeath you the legacy of my parents.

To Julie Kroll for her undaunted spirit, kindness, and love.

And to Maxine Olove, who has guided me on the path to enlightenment, I am grateful.

CONTENTS

INTRODUCTION

M ost of us select a life partner who is unknown to our family and friends. This means it is up to us alone to discern whether the person we've fallen in love with is the right one, the one with whom we really can spend a lifetime. Unfortunately, in the heat of passion self-preserving mechanisms sometimes get turned off, and we make disastrous mistakes. Many people, in fact, make the same mistakes again and again, because they don't look before they love.

Look Before You Love reveals how a personal environment is an expression of a person's emotional inner being; how choices for a home reveal as much about someone as personality. Filtered through a body of knowledge known as *feng shui*, this book shows how taking a close look at the art forms, colors, objects, and furniture styles in a new love's home can give you a profound understanding of that man or woman that would normally take years to unveil.

It always takes two to form a lifetime partnership, of course. Maybe what has been lacking in your choices of love is an understanding of yourself. This book can help you look more deeply at the patterns that emerge from your own home choices and the messages those patterns send to prospective partners. I've met many people who long for a companion but live in a space arranged strictly for one. I've known others who choose the wrong mates because they don't understand their own inner selves and what role their core being plays in forming enduring partnerships. I've encountered many others whose relationships end up in trouble because they don't realize how great an influence their home environment has on the success or failure of their love. The principles in this book can help you surmount all of these problems.

Feng shui investigates how who we are is influenced by where we are. Approximately six thousand years ago feng shui originated in China as an outgrowth of studies of climate, topography, geology, and vegetation that enabled the Chinese to evaluate a setting and determine what conditions were optimal for thriving. According to feng shui, our personal environment, including the placement of furnishings and artifacts, the use of color, and architectural details, can inspire success or doom us to failure. In this book I have applied that premise to love, examining how selection of physical objects reveals dimensions of a lover's inner self that are hard to fathom in the early stages of any relationship.

In my first three books on feng shui, I sought to unravel feng shui from its esoteric roots and translate its enlightened messages into a model for the contemporary Western lifestyle and philosophy. In doing so, I formulated the pyramid school of feng shui, which uses biology, cultural anthropology, and psychology as well as the body of knowledge gleaned from many physical sciences, to support the ancient concepts and rules, stripped of cultural influences. The pyramid school allows those of us who are not Chinese or versed in Eastern cultural or philosophical systems to apply our own values and aesthetics to the essence of traditional feng shui. It gives all of us access to the wisdom provided by an understanding of how and why our physical environment influences us.

Fundamentally, pyramid feng shui evaluates how we respond to stimuli and suggests ways to improve the ongoing interaction with our environment. A rather simple example of such a response is our instinctive avoidance of adverse physical contact with objects bigger, stronger, and faster than we are, which we experience as threatening. Feng shui seeks to use and strengthen biological response systems like these that have helped us survive as a species. Massive, towering objects, such as tall buildings across from a home or high furniture positioned close to a chair can feel uncomfortable or diminish our capacity to tackle a task at hand. Blocking the view of a large building with a plant and obscuring the view of a large piece of furniture by repositioning a chair are easy ways to correct basic problems posed by our biological response systems. In this book we'll be aiming more specifically at improving the interaction of our physical environment with the intimate relationships we desire.

Whether you use feng shui to create a generally beneficial environment or to nurture a lasting relationship, more than biological response systems play a role in what works. The cultural rules for appropriate responses will vary depending on your background and cannot be omitted from any study of your interaction with your environment. What is polite and appropriate in one culture could be disrespectful and way out of line in another. We learn how to act based on the rules that exist in our communities. The pyramid school therefore allows you to adapt feng shui for cultural differences. It also allows you to understand another's cultural influences better by interpreting his or her choices for an environment.

Personal genetics are another variable that determines in part how we respond to stimuli. We have all been told many times that there never has been and never will be another person exactly the same as us. Because of this complexity, there are naturally many parts of every person that are left unarticulated. Feng shui is one way to peer into those parts and gain a greater understanding of each unique individual. The principles of this ancient discipline tell us that the choice of a square glass-topped coffee table may suggest a person who is reliable, while a dark wooden square table might expose a streak of stubbornness. They explain why armless chairs in a main gathering room suggest someone who might be more at ease alone.

Why are we attracted to one object and not another? The answer to this question is revealed partly by understanding our basic elemental self. Our unique experiences in life bend us toward one choice and not another. We are lured by and feel comfortable with certain objects and not others. It is uncanny how furniture, color, and art objects match the basic nature of the person who chooses them. Those with fiery personalities often have many fire symbols throughout their home, and those who are whirlwinds of activity often have a plethora of metal elemental images in their home. We tend to select colors, shapes, and patterns that concur with either our expressed personality or our more elusive emotional nature. We tend to live with things that express who we are.

Who are we? That is a burning question for most of us. Understanding the layers of self is a feat not unlike rescuing someone from a stampeding crowd. Being fully integrated in a deep down-to-the-bones sense is the work of a lifetime. Too often we accept a shadow version of ourselves, one that is incomplete or inappropriately selective. To the outsider this shadow self is indistinguishable from the real person. But by examining choices made in the physical world, we can begin to determine whether the outward expression of a person matches his or her true nature.

We select objects because our emotional centers reverberate with them. If you have ever gasped with delight when viewing a painting, you have experienced the full power of how an object can elicit an emotional response. You react intensely to an inanimate object because it embodies who you are as much as your personality does.

While the conscious mind puts thoughts into words to communicate, emotions can be expressed through actions and choices. We all live with things that express us. What surrounds each of us is in many ways a replica of us. When you can interpret someone's choices, a fuller understanding of that person emerges.

Shirley is a good example. Her selection of artwork spanned a range of color, texture, line, and material. She owned wood, metal, macramé sculpture; abstract, realistic, superrealistic, surrealistic paintings; and artifacts of every conceivable shape, size, and ethnicity. It would be impossible to describe her home as having a single color scheme; every color of the rainbow was represented. The effect was neither confusing nor chaotic but stunning.

Despite the apparent lack of a unifying color scheme, there were certain themes in Shirley's home if you looked closely enough. The greater majority of the images were strong women: a steel dancer, macramé statues, carved Amazon warriors, and paintings of women of many races and cultures, dancing, marching, resting, or simply being alluring. Upon contemplation, I realized that this theme fitted her perfectly. Shirley was, after all, a woman of considerable talents. It seemed that whatever she endeavored to do was realized. Capable females engaging in compelling activities was the consistent message her artwork exposed.

Have you ever visited the home of a business colleague and been startled by what you saw? When messages from one setting seem to contradict those from another, it doesn't mean one of them is false. We often see segments of a person in one setting that are not apparent in another simply because all aspects of self are not always appropriate in all settings.

What is telling is whether some thread connects what is seen, what is felt, and what is heard. When there is discord in the environment, there may be discord within the person. Which one causes the other is not really important. What is important is that a cherished goal might never be achieved.

On my jaunt around America pitching my first feng shui book, I was invited to stay at the home of a thirty-nine-year-old female friend. I was touched when she announced she would relinquish her bedroom to help me spend a comfortable night. After we had wolfed down bowls of ice cream late into the night and shared our life's dreams, I toddled into her bedroom and flopped, exhausted, onto her childhood's single bed and listened to the reverberations my arrival made on the clanky metal headboard.

Tucking my hands palms up under my head, I surveyed the bedroom and was struck by what I saw. Because she had confided to me that she longed to get married, the room's furnishings revealed a picture of my friend of which I had not been entirely conscious. She was using her bedroom as a home owner uses a cellar. To the right of the bed a broken television perched ominously. Straight ahead was a vacuum cleaner, its retrieval bag deflated like a helium balloon the morning after a party. With only one small artifact on the walls and a central overhead fixture, the atmosphere exuded a transient quality, making it hard to believe she had occupied this apartment for more than four years. The drapes hung listlessly from a pole, and the overall color scheme was dull and dry. Boy, I thought, no wonder she had never married. I could only imagine the unconscious messages telegraphed to potential suitors who viewed this space.

Did a single bed, broken television, household appliance, and lack of memorabilia reflect my friend's real desires? Not as I knew them. Instead they seemed to express feelings of inadequacy, feelings that didn't come through in her overt self. She is as appealing as a Norman Rockwell painting, has a secure job in university administration, and is kind, caring, and sweet. But if they came to her home, potential suitors might see her as colorless and barely keeping it together.

The next morning I shared my interpretation with her, hoping it would propel her to change the bedroom to reflect a more accurate picture of her, thereby attracting a person who would be appropriate.

Get a double bed, I told her, and fix or discard the broken television. In its place put a glorious bedside lamp. Purchase a colorful bedspread, rehang the curtain rod, and dye the drapes to match one upbeat color on the new bedspread. She followed my advice and is presently moving into a new house purchased with her new male companion. Did the change alter her, or did her home reflect an outmoded self? I don't really know, nor is it important to figure out which came first, the chicken or the egg. I do know that our state of mind influences our environment and that our environment in turn affects our internal state.

This experience began my investigation into how interiors reveal who we are and how changing them can revamp both our view of the world and how the world views us. For the next couple of years, I became a home sleuth. Without knowing it, I sought to identify things in a home that could tell a story or reveal an essence. Sometimes this helped me work with my clients, who were amazed that I was able to unearth their inner feelings. Sometimes it sped me down a troublesome road where I was flung headfirst into their resistance. Finally, I knew that a home could be a tool to help implement personal change when a person was ready.

That change can take the form of making better choices in love by learning how to read an individual's environment. It can take shape as altering your environment so that a physical change can be the inspiration for an internal one. When my friend was ready to change her bedroom, her insecurities, manifested by a less-than-aesthetic bedroom, were visibly cast away and removed as a crutch to lean on. Essentially this book is a tool for learning more about yourself and another who is important to you. A home expresses its occupant's outward personality as well as hidden emotional content.

Feng shui offers us a guide to help illuminate our own and others' qualities. By categorizing personalities into elements, each with its own characteristics, we have a way to understand how someone else's inner and outer selves fit or do not fit with ours—who is likely to be compatible or not. If you already have a partner, discerning his or her essential nature and how to dovetail it with yours will be a benefit to a long-term relationship.

At the heart of this book are the premises that all physical objects represent one of the five elements—fire, earth, metal, water, and wood—that these five elements are archetypes categorizing human nature, and that we select for our homes those elements that represent who we are. You may have described a person as fiery, solid as a rock, or slippery and already have intuitively grasped the meaning of each element. This book will delve deeply into the basic positive and challenging characteristics of the elements, how these characteristics manifest themselves in humans, and how they influence behavior. For example, if you are nervous before a date, the color blue can help you relax. If you feel exasperated by a loved one's clutter, you can help him or her think about change by introducing the wood element into a home. If you are struck speechless every time a particular person visits with you, adding a silver frame mirror in a room can help ideas surface.

Sometimes intention alone is enough to produce change. Called the Heidelberg principle, this phenomenon states that the mere fact of being observed changes its results. Gary Zukav, in his book *The Dancing Wu Li Masters,* explains it thus: ". . . At the subatomic level, we cannot observe something without changing it. . . . The physical properties which we observe in the external world are enmeshed in our perceptions not only psychologically, but ontologically as well." This is good news and helps explain why, when we desire change, the mere fact of focusing our attention on the desire helps make it come true. I often am told after a feng shui consultation that the hoped-for changes start materializing immediately, as if by magic. Checks arrive in the mail the next day, a sought-after partner calls within a few hours, or an inattentive student suddenly buckles down soon after I depart. I attribute this in part to the Heidelberg principle.

Quantum mechanics states that there are two possibilities at the onset of an event. When the reality presents itself to those observing, the other possibility ceases to exist. Good news for those seeking change. When positive change begins to manifest, the negative side ceases to exist.

I am grateful to be part of an intellectual and political system that allows unrestricted exploration. I am indebted to my family and friends who have inspired me to dare to inquire. In some ways I feel as if I am standing on the edge of an ocean of truths. Soon others will follow and substantiate these and other concepts in ways I haven't even fathomed. To the extent that we can learn to live with our own nature and that of the ones we choose to love, I gladly open a path of inquiry and let the future shape it.

> *Best future relationships!*
> *With love,*
> *Nancilee Wydra*

Part 1

WHO I AM AND WHO I THINK I AM

1

ARE YOU READY FOR LOVE?

Happiness is bolstered by having loved ones and being loved. Many of us are fortunate enough to have a whole tier of people on whom we rely as well as dote. Children, parents, siblings, and friends fill our lives with ongoing joy and peace of mind. Yet without a life partner we often feel bereft. As we have evolved, the biological drive to find a mate has remained strong. And at least in contemporary Western societies, the notion of romantic love as a euphoric state of ecstasy makes finding the love of our life seem even more urgent.

Haste and high expectations may be why we make so many mistakes. We see a new love through rose-colored glasses and want to believe our beloved is beyond reproach. During this early phase, we view our beloved as he or she will never be seen again. Many of us wait for the one who will sweep us off our feet, make bells ring, cause us to swoon, and respond to us instantly and accurately. The problem is that those we meet are well aware of such expectations and might at the onset try hard to meet them. Thus the person we meet and fall in love with is often a fabrication. It's not necessarily dishonesty but just the game we all believe we have to play to find and win a lover.

Unfortunately the game often ends with us feeling that the person we love has transformed into an object of distaste. We are completely surprised and disappointed. It doesn't have to be that way. In order to see beyond what we are told, we need to use a system that cannot be manipulated or camouflaged. The choices we make are like lie detectors; they reveal the truth because we have no control over our automatic responses to what we naturally choose to surround ourselves within our homes. Feng shui can be that conduit to the truth, because we generally do not filter our choices of furnishings and artwork, and they, like the printout from a lie detector, are apt to reveal the truth. When we feel an affinity for certain styles and an aversion for others, we are responding to an internal voice that cannot lie.

Statistics claim that every time a relationship fails, the chances increase exponentially that the next partnership will fail. Only when you choose to discriminate based on some credible, discernible criteria do you stand a chance of succeeding in forming an untroubled alliance. But before you can use feng shui to see beyond a potential lover's words, you should apply it to your own desire for love. You say you're ready for love, but what does your internal voice say? Answer *yes* or *no* to the following questions.

ARE YOU READY FOR LOVE?

1. Are the closets in your home filled to overflowing?

2. Is there ample space for new books on bookshelves?

3. Do you have night tables on both sides of your bed?

4. Have you piled things you use on both night tables?

5. Do you have adequate lighting on both sides of your bed?

6. Do you have available a spare robe, gloves, or sweater not necessarily in your size?

7. Do you have special wines, liquors, cigars, or chocolates for company?

8. Did you decline the call-waiting option for your telephone?

9. Do pets sleep in your bed?

10. Do you have a few seating groups for two throughout your home?

If you answered *yes* to questions 1, 4, 8, and 9, you are not that desirous of having a relationship. If you insist that this is not true, empty a closet, train your pets to sleep on their own beds or the floor, and call up the telephone company and have call waiting installed.

If you answered *yes* to questions 2, 3, 5, 6, 7, and 10, then you are sincerely ready for love. There is a saying that a guru appears only when you are ready. So it is that the journey will begin only when you are ready.

2

EXPLORING
THE BRAIN

How much do you know about yourself? Most people believe they know themselves quite well. But if the quiz in Chapter 1 showed you are not as ready for love as you thought, this question should give you pause. Is it possible that you don't know yourself any better than you know the person you're falling in love with? Sometimes we buy our own advertising, convincing ourselves that the facade we put out there in the first blush of romantic love is the real thing. Deep down most of us know that charm is not substance, that self-image is not the same thing as self-confidence. But if what you show to others, what you express in words is not all there is to you, who are you?

Answering that question is a lifelong process, of course, but unless you know something about your inner self, you can hardly expect a relationship to blossom. In this chapter we'll take a brief look at the phenomenal human brain and how its workings govern the way we respond—to people, places, and events in our environment. The next chapter will explore some fundamental aspects of self and how similarities in them between you and a prospective partner can make a relationship while differences may break it.

The unfolding of conscious awareness from birth or the way we learn to interpret the extraordinary amount of impulses our brain receives and transmits is a success story of the same magnitude as the emergence of life on this planet. To understand why we respond to stimuli in particular ways, we have to know a few facts about the operation of the human brain.

The three main areas in the brain are the brain stem, midbrain, and cortex, each with different responsibilities for our well-being and functioning.

The brain stem regulates basic life functions automatically. We don't need to think consciously in order to breathe, pump blood, ingest food, or instigate stereotypical responses, like grimacing when disgusted, widening the eyes when surprised, or clenching a fist when angry. These responses or functions are controlled automatically by the brain stem.

The midbrain or limbic system is the emotional center of the brain. In the same way that being hugged and describing a hug are different, the midbrain experiences emotional reactions and can by interpreting the emotions of others help us discern how they feel. The midbrain creates and interprets the emotional dramas going on all around us. Daniel Goleman writes in his book *Emotional Intelligence* that social deftness, motivation, impulse control, and persistence are all the responsibilities of a part of the brain that has little to do with the brain's center, which is measured by standard IQ tests. This emotional knowingness is accessed not by conscious thought but by what we call *intuition*.

I knew my neighbor Lydia for more than ten years when she bounded up my front steps just as I was leaving home. In the nanoseconds it took for her to travel the distance from the bottom of the steps to the door, I knew something was amiss, even though not one word had been spoken. Her first words, "I need a witch's brew for anxiety," did not catch me off guard. How did I know in that instant that something was wrong? Perhaps her speed was atypically hurried, her eyes were slightly distended, or her mouth slightly agape, triggering this knowingness. Our capacity for empathy and understanding is an important filter through which we view our surroundings.

This story, coupled with perhaps thousands of your own, underscores how humans react to stimuli instantly without translating what is experienced into words. Without effort or rational thought, the emotional center of the brain reacts to events.

In the same way as we respond to people emotionally, we respond to objects. Objects take on implicit emotional meaning based on material, shape, color, and content. We select one painting over another because it speaks to our soul, which means it supports or stimulates an inner connection. Why we choose art objects, colors, prints, flooring, furniture styles, etc., has to do less with our pocketbooks and more with our emotional selves. Objects express emotions more than words can, because we don't necessarily articulate feelings into language. Considering that we spend far more time feeling than we do thinking or speaking, as Goleman points out, objects chosen for a home reflect a substantial part of our inner selves.

Before we share our lives with another or when we are trying to smooth out the bumps in a present relationship, learning to interpret our emotional reactions can help uncover hidden aspects of how we feel.

This principle helped me understand my friends Barbara and Harry, who, despite having been married for a dozen years and having a child, live in a home that looks like it was furnished by newlyweds. Although they both have well-paying jobs, their furniture is mostly hand-me-downs. The bamboo sofa with its brightly colored cotton cover probably last graced the porch of a relative's home. Another armless sofa has cushions that slide out from under when sat upon, and benches instead of chairs surround their dining room table. All in all there are no furnishings that invite you to hang out. Their gathering space tweaked emotions not unlike ones I had during my youth when comfort was hardly a criteria.

The implied impermanence of both the porch furniture and the picnic benches transmitted the idea of two persons who didn't want to take their adult responsibilities seriously. My interpretation was substantiated when Harry chose a job so far away that he was able to come home only on weekends. Barbara and her daughter had a relationship similar to two girlfriends, and the lack of both a husband and a father appeared not to matter. And why would a married couple with plenty of expendable income choose furniture meant to be outside? Barbara and Harry had accepted living in a marriage that was both outside customary boundaries and likely to erode, as does outdoor furniture.

What can the brain reveal about you? In his book *Beyond the Conscious Mind*, Thomas Blakeslee discusses Nobel laureate Gerald Edelman's theory of neural Darwinism, which states that the brain is a cluster of complex modules of cognition. The two areas of the brain, simply explained as the emotional system (limbic) and the thinking system (neocortex), apparently organize their responses to outside stimuli in these modules. Each module works independently, yet many modules can respond simultaneously to a situation in the same way as, when we see a child in danger, our feet, body, hands, and voice operate in unison to rescue the child. As in any efficient large corporation, tasks are divided and delegated to individual modules, yet individual modules can associate with each other.

Picture the brain's module as a paper bag filled with tiny dots. These dots are potentials that when used will reach out and connect with other dots in patterns that when repeated become entrenched behaviors. Our experiences influence the patterns. The more we repeat a pattern, the more fixed it becomes. As we get older, the patterns in each module typically become harder to break.

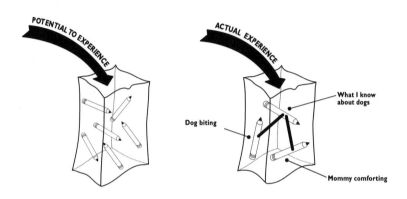

Before an experience a module has only potential;
after an experience it starts developing a pattern.

Consider this scenario. A dog approaches and bites a child's hand. This creates a module we'll call "What I Know About Dogs." One day the child is playing in a sandbox, a dog comes into view, and the child panics. The module begins to signal the child to be frightened of being bitten. At that moment the child is helpless to alter her feelings.

Can a traumatic experience ever be altered? The human brain has an uncanny way of switching modules. Let's say the same child has a module entitled "Pleasant Experience with Cats." Because both dogs and cats are furry, four-legged creatures, the child's brain might switch to that module upon the next encounter with a dog; the child might believe that this time the furry creature will act more like a cat. If the dog does *not* bite this time, the "What I Know About Dogs" module will have a positive experience superimposed over it. The original experience about dogs is not completely erased but obscured by a newer, more positive one, and it remains underneath the scrawl of other experiences, ready to exert its influence on the child's life, perhaps in a strange and seemingly random manner.

Each experience reinforces a module's niche, locking in the way a person will respond to a given situation with similar variables. Modules program how we view stimuli from the outside world. The module that is called the *self* or *introspection module* absorbs the first awareness of how we are perceived by others. This module is the one we use when we think about ourselves.

While independent from other clusters, the self module perceives itself to be the one that "embodies" all others. The likelihood that this self module is able to correctly discern or control what all the other brain modules are doing and feeling is, however, as likely as one person single-handedly stopping a rioting crowd. Therefore, our notion of self is not as cohesive and all-pervasive as we think it is. Simply put, the self module believes it has access to all parts of ourselves when in fact it is merely one in a series of modules that interprets and addresses who we are and how we feel about ourselves.

Like different parts of an automobile's motor, each module operates alone and at the same time as all others. Our mind is like a room full of students taking a test simultaneously. During the same time frame, each searches for answers through his or her own learning experiences. Thus the brain functions together yet is compartmentalized through individuating modules.

The notion of self is a shared activity by many various parts of the brain that have no access to each other. We are composed of a fraternity of modules that hopefully, like a collegiate social group, have something in common and are compatible with each other. Gerald Edelman unveiled the knowledge that when a new situation arises and previous learning is of no help, a new cluster may be formed. Yet modules can be at odds with each other and fight for the right to be expressed. Naturally only one wins, and the winner in a way has tricked us into believing that its pattern is the appropriate one.

The self module gives rise to the self-perception that is translated into words. This module is located in the cerebral cortex, the only part of the brain that uses symbols called *words* to construct information. The neocortex, as the seat of thought, comprehends and puts together what the senses perceive. Humans' highly developed neocortex has added greatly to the survival of the species because it has a talent for strategizing and planning and endows us with mental agility. It's no wonder then that we hold thinking in high esteem and believe it is the primary vehicle that expresses self. *Unfortunately, the part of the brain that uses words thinks it can understand and give voice to all of our experiences. This is a false belief.*

Our choices, such as those for our homes, articulate experiences of those modules seated in the nonverbal, emotional parts of our brain. In observing and interpreting an environment, we concentrate on the modules that express self in ways other than words or thoughts. If you attend a gallery opening and are enthralled by one piece of art, your passion for this work initially enters your consciousness as a pleasant feeling or enthusiasm. Only later are you able to put this emotion into words. The choices we make in our homes express parts of our self that are unexpressed by words. They come from our emotional centers and are usually not accessible to our intellectual processes. Observing choices can be more reliable than listening to words.

3

THE NOTION
OF SELF

We Westerners believe in a separate self, an "I" that stands apart from our being that is part of a family, tribe, religion, and ecosystem. This notion of self would seem bizarre in many other cultures, where each person is considered only part of a greater, seamless whole. While you may very well find a life partner from your own culture, an important part of looking before you love is understanding how the notion of self may vary among those you meet, whether they adhere to a cultural tradition different from your own or reflect a unique American blend. Components of self that seem to play a great role in relationships include the amount of control we believe we have over our destiny, the boundaries of self, and how we perceive time.

> **Three important self-concepts are the amount of control we believe we have over our destiny, the boundaries of self, and how we perceive time.**

CONTROL

"I can do it," is a basic premise drilled into Westerners. The Horatio Alger image of the young man steeled to travel west to seek fortune and fame has been ingrained in our psyches. Young Alger is expected to overcome daunting odds and face, alone and ingeniously, whatever challenges are set before him. He is expected to control his destiny.

The Western notion of control—that what we do will affect what happens—is unique. Based on this notion, we are generally taught to curb our innate response systems to spawn some positive consequence. An example is postponing gratification to reach long-term goals. Although sacrificing for one's progeny does seem to have some biological benefits, the Western concept of control seems to be learned and is not common to all cultures or subcultures in this country. In fact, well-established institutions such as Alcoholics Anonymous and Weight Watchers bend the notion of the self in control. Assigning buddies and setting up supportive meetings are acknowledgment that the self is not actually in complete control.

Though the people you form relationships with will probably espouse an attitude about control that falls somewhere in the realm between Horatio Alger and Weight Watchers, the range of possibilities is much broader. On one end of the spectrum of the self-in-control are the Tibetan Buddhists, who believe the mind is responsible for all personal reality. By intention steeled through chanting, people can transform their lives and obliterate pain and suffering. The self or, in this case, mind is the tool that produces change. On the other end of the spectrum lie the indigenous Dinka people inhabiting the Nile River region of Africa. The Dinkas essentially have no concept of individualized self. They do not think about themselves in relation to events or even to what is happening to them at any moment. Unlike us, they have no mechanism for storing up experiences of self to reflect on past experiences. What they did yesterday has essentially no bearing on what is happening today. Life experience is not ingested as something to be used for self-awareness or self-growth at a later date. What is happening is not a reflection of "who I am" but simply of the moment and the whim of the gods.

Where do you fall on this spectrum? Marsha and Larry illustrate how inhabiting different points on the spectrum can cause conflict in a relationship. Marsha and Larry married late in life. Marsha had just embarked on a new career when they met. Her enthusiasm and energy were consistent with her belief that with hard work and a little luck she could accomplish what she desired, which in her case was deciding she wanted to be an actress in her midforties. Marsha believed she had some control over how she was perceived and therefore did fairly well in her new profession. Larry, on the other hand, was forced to change careers because his former employer sold out to a large company and his job as salesman was eliminated. He believed that at his age (late forties) few other companies would hire him. Consequently, he interviewed for jobs offering only commission or in which he, the employee, had to purchase the product for resale. Although he never questioned his salesmanship, he felt no control over his destiny and accepted one marginal sales job after another. Marsha and Larry acted extremely differently based on their personal notion of control and time. Marsha believed she herself was in control, and Larry believed others controlled him. Their vastly different attitudes affected not only the outcome of their work lives but their personal lives as well. Larry thought Marsha was lucky, and Marsha thought Larry had a defeatist attitude. Their divergent beliefs were a major reason why their marriage disintegrated. Naturally it is better to be with someone whose beliefs match yours.

Answer the following questions to determine how you view the self in control.

WHO IS IN CONTROL OF YOUR LIFE?

1. If my high school had been more academically rigorous, I would have

   a. gone to college.
   b. read the classics.
   c. had less time for socializing.
   d. none of the above.

2. I am generally late for parties or other social appointments because

   a. I don't plan my time appropriately.
   b. traffic is usually heavy.
   c. I tend to get lost.
   d. I often get phone calls or have people drop by just before I leave.

3. I forgot to send a card on a friend's birthday because

   a. I was extremely busy at work.
   b. I forgot to write it down in my day planner.
   c. she missed my birthday.
   d. I am not as thoughtful as I should be.

4. I do not return calls left on my answering machine

    a. when I know they will ask me to contribute to a charity.

    b. because I don't want to talk to that person.

    c. because I am busy with activities I like.

    d. only when I can't make out the name and number.

5. If I am asked to contribute to a cause and don't want to, I usually

    a. say I have already distributed all my yearly charity allotments.

    b. say I am not interested in that particular charity enough to contribute.

    c. cave in and donate something.

    d. say I have personal pressing financial needs, even when it is not true.

If you gave these answers, you believe you are in control: 1, d; 2, a or c; 3, b or d; 4, c or d; 5, b. If you gave these answers, you believe others are in control: 1, a, b, or c; 2, b or d; 3, a or c; 4, a or b; 5, a, c, or d.

Boundaries

Edward T. Hall, eminent cultural anthropologist, points out the vastly different patterns and criteria different groups of people have regarding distance. Have you ever traveled abroad and felt uncomfortable when someone stood too close? How close we stand next to another is so ingrained that we think about it only when face-to-face with someone who has crossed our comfort boundaries.

> **What defines personal space and when it is invaded is learned early in childhood and is rarely thought about consciously.**

I was fifteen years old when I came face-to-face with cultural distancing. I had been invited to spend time abroad with my aunt and uncle in Madrid, when Spain was ruled by a dictator and evening curfews were imposed. At 9:00 P.M. all citizens but Los Tunas, a roving band of male university musicians whose serenades drifted into the homes and hearts of local residents, were allowed to wander unchallenged throughout the silent streets.

One evening during dinner in my relatives' second-floor apartment, the strains of guitar music floated through an open window. My aunt jumped up, clutched my arm, and escorted me out onto the balcony. There, directly under the cantilevered balcony, were six or seven dashing young men in long, billowing black velvet capes performing an amazing melody. So enthralled was I that I barely noticed my aunt dashing back inside to retrieve long, thin colorful ribbons. "Throw these to your favorites," she urged. The next few minutes were spent combating my shyness and tossing ribbons to several young men below. With heart racing, I returned inside to continue dinner.

Within moments there was a pounding on the front door. My uncle leaped up from the table, opened the door, and framed in the threshold was a heart-stopping sight. The musicians were coming inside! Dizzy with ecstasy, I eased out of the chair and found myself completely surrounded by these dashing young men. Within minutes panic set in, because they had all crossed my boundary of comfort. I could feel their breath, smell what they had had for dinner, and regard their faces at a distance that was in my culture reserved for kissing. Ecstasy converted to distress. My comfort zone had been penetrated, and the romance of the evening was extinguished.

We consider our possessions an extension of self.

The concept of boundaries extends to possessions too. I, not unlike many children, had favorite objects such as teddy bears, blankets, books, or dolls that I found it hard to be without. When I went off to kindergarten, a piece of my favorite blanket went with me. It was inconceivable to me to be anywhere without my security blanket. Westerners are very attached to possessions, which represent comfort or value or add importance to the sense of self.

In other cultures possessions do not have such a pervasive influence on the sense of self. The descendants of Guatemala's Mayan Indians, for example, do not even individualize their clothing. Every village has a unique costume for its male and female members. Every year the women of the village weave a fresh outfit for family members that is styled exactly the same for every other member of the village. No matter what their age or station, all females and males wear one style of outfit from birth until death.

WHICH BOUNDARIES ARE MOST IMPORTANT TO YOU?

1. I feel responsible for my children

    a. when they are at home.
    b. until they are finished with their education.
    c. until they are married.
    d. for their entire lives.

2. If a member of my immediate family commited a crime, I would

    a. feel as if I were in some way responsible.
    b. consider how the person may not be fulfilled by his or her career.
    c. consider the neighborhood's influences a contributing factor.
    d. know that some people are born to be bad.

3. When I travel, I normally take

    a. far too many clothes.
    b. an alarm clock even if I know that the hotel will likely have one.
    c. a favorite soap, shampoo, or pillow.
    d. a lucky icon.

4. I would be most devastated if I lost in a fire

    a. my clothing.
    b. my books.
    c. my furniture.
    d. my art.

5. I would feel most uncomfortable

    a. in a crowded subway.
    b. sharing an office.
    c. sitting at a lunch counter.
    d. living as an adult with my parents.

6. I would never

    a. go outside without completing my morning toiletry.
    b. skip reading the morning paper or listening to the morning news.
    c. go to the supermarket in a dirty or frayed outfit.
    d. go where I am not invited.

7. I typically

    a. buy a new outfit for any wedding I am invited to.
    b. dress for success.
    c. don't wear old or worn-out clothes outside the house.
    d. buy the most comfortable night wear.

There are four boundaries of self: physical, intellectual, social, and emotional. The physical boundary is most important to you if you answered 1a, 2d, 3a, 4a, 5a, 6a, and 7d. The intellectual boundary is most important to you if you answered 1b, 2b, 3b, 4b, 5c, 6b, and 7b. The social boundary is most important to you if you answered 1c, 2c, 3c, 4d, 5b, 6c, and 7c. The emotional boundary is most important to you if you answered 1d, 2a, 3d, 4c, 5d, 6d, and 7a.

Physical

Those who see their body as primarily an asset or a liability will have more answers in the physical category. Concerned with their physical appearance, they feel judged by how others experience them. In gaining acceptance, people whose boundaries do not extend much beyond their physical body will focus intensely on their appearance. This type keeps plastic surgeons working and gyms filled.

Intellectual

Knowledge is their most valued possession. These people feel judged by how smart they are and seek the company of those who will appreciate their intelligence. They relate to others verbally, not kinesthetically or visually.

Social

When appropriate behavior is important to you, you will select more answers in this category. Your definition of self is formed by how others perceive your social status.

Jean and Stuart retired to Florida from Arkansas. They rented a home in a prestigious neighborhood, and Stuart became depressed. Stuart, who had built up a successful practice as a litigation attorney winning many cases that captured national attention, felt as if he were unknown in his new home. He had thrived on being appreciated for his achievements but no longer knew people who automatically knew of his work. His sense of self, which was attached to his intellectual accomplishments, had to be rebuilt in his new hometown.

Emotional

When feelings are used as boundaries between what is important and what is not, emotions take precedence over other attributes. These people value how they feel or how they make others feel before anything else and will not want to be engaged in a superficial relationship or have acquaintances in lieu of friends.

As we were driving away from a humane society luncheon meeting, a friend of mine remarked about a woman who had sat next to us. In the first four minutes of conversation, we heard about eighteen discourses on how she felt about everything from the speaker to the food served.

"Oh my gosh," my friend Deborah remarked, "could you stand her?" I mumbled the beginning of a response, but before I could finish a sentence she went on. "I couldn't stand her! Who cares how she feels? Did you notice she had absolutely nothing to say about the new project?" Apparently, our table mate was invested in her emotional life and was connecting with us via emotions, which was not Deborah's first line of connection in a social situation.

Valuing one aspect of self over another can lead to anguish when those in our lives do not hold the same aspect of self in esteem.

TIME

Are you old yet? I felt grown up at twelve and young at forty! Culture teaches us how to feel about aging. In China being older guarantees being wiser, while here we experience aging as accompanied by a loss of attractiveness and control. Moreover, Westerners think of time as a commodity. It can be saved, stored, wasted, or controlled. The field of time management implies that time is a tool and can be manipulated.

Ram Das, a New Age guru, startled us with the notion that we should be here now. I often ask attendees of my classes to write down three things that presently trouble them. The list of worries often includes concerns about not having enough money to retire, hoping to find a mate, or desiring to improve life's status in some way. Worrying about the future implies the notion of control over time.

For most of human history, people were not viewed as stewards of time. One generation was not expected to vary too greatly from the next. Children followed in the footsteps of parents. Time was not always synonymous with gains or changes.

Today we are hard pressed not to change. With few exceptions, most of us do not live in the town where we were born. We believe that time and change are inevitable. In a culture where relaxation is viewed as the opportunity to better oneself at a hobby or sport, time is a commodity to be used for self-improvement. In a world that considers instant communication standard, the linear movement of time is speeding up. Time as a personal commodity is ingrained in the Western notion of self.

Westerners consider time a commodity to be manipulated.

Couples who have vastly different views of time often clash. My parents taught me that if you weren't five minutes early, you were late. Their world had clear limits with regard to time, and they believed that you could control time and not let it control you. My father actually only worked nine to five; my mother was always home weekdays at 11:45 to serve us lunch. I don't think that they ever felt that time could not be controlled except when we were in traffic. My parents experienced traffic as enormously distressful, partly because in it they could not manage time. Living with someone who feels time can be controlled can be taxing to someone who does not. The controller of time would be frustrated with the one who was casual about time and vice versa. It would be frustrating to me to live with someone who was less than punctual. It is far better to be with someone whose view of time is similar to yours or to have an understanding of how it may be different.

How Do You View Time?

1. I get up early

    a. to accomplish a great deal.
    b. so I will not feel rushed.
    c. only if I have slept enough to stay healthy.

2. I like to plan in detail

    a. how my day will be spent.
    b. for my retirement.
    c. how to get to a new location.

3. I tend to worry about

    a. whether I will remain healthy when I am old.
    b. when I will die.
    c. whether I will be able to work long enough to have a financially secure old age.

4. If I know I will be late, I usually

    a. rush even more.
    b. contact the person waiting for me to say I will be late.
    c. cut short what I am doing to leave earlier.

5. I am

    a. rarely late.
    b. careful to spend time with only those I like.
    c. interested in having the most fun possible.

This test determines whether time has value to you—you feel time is like a commodity and is either valuable or not; time can be controlled—you believe time can be controlled or managed; or time is limited—you feel time is limited and therefore what you do has vast long-term repercussions. If you answered 1a, 2a, 3c, 4b, and 5b, you value time. If you answered 1b, 2c, 3a, 4c, and 5a, you believe time can be controlled. If you answered 1c, 2b, 3b, 4a, and 5c, you feel time is limited.

Although these three views of time are not mutually exclusive, one typically has a tendency to value one over the other. When, as an adult, I realized my parents' hysterics about being caught in traffic stemmed from the high value they placed on controlling time, I became more patient with their outbursts.

The self is commingled with cultural considerations. We must think about these differences, especially now that a multicultural life experience is becoming more the norm than the exception. How you experience relationships is in part influenced by how you view time and what values are associated with your notion of self.

Part II

BASICS OF
FENG SHUI

4

FENG SHUI: COMMUNICATING WITH YOUR ENVIRONMENT

F eng shui describes the communication that takes place every day between you and an environment. Although the Chinese words *feng shui* mean "wind and water," this discipline investigates the universal feelings and reactions of human beings to an environment. The teachings of feng shui explore how connections (Tao), balance (yin and yang), and vitality (chi) can impact positively on life; how the senses of sight, sound, smell, and touch deeply influence behavior. Consider, for example, trying to finish an urgent report one summer day from a desk that faces the blinding afternoon sun. You might rush through or be distracted and not do the best job possible because the setting sun interferes with your concentration. The poor report might affect a potential promotion or raise. Sometimes one adverse physical detail can have profound long-term effects. This principle applies to your love life as well as your work life, of course, and that is what this book is all about.

Feng shui investigates the universal feelings and reactions of human beings to an environment.

An environment affects all aspects of life, and you may see evidence of it in family relationships, spiritually, and even health. A love life, an integral part of what makes life grand, can benefit from feng shui techniques. The common cold as well as more life-threatening diseases such as cancer, Alzheimer's disease, multiple sclerosis, and AIDS can, in some cases, be improved or experienced as less devastating when changes are made in a living space. Feng shui does not cure but can remove obstacles in an environment that impact detrimentally on a disease. For example, removing the shine from a floor can help a person with multiple sclerosis walk with greater confidence. Surrounding a cancer patient with yellow flowers can be an adjunct to radiation since yellow is associated with detoxification. I hope you will remain open to the many insights feng shui can bring into your life.

> **Feng shui is more about how one experiences place than place itself.**

In this chapter I offer a brief overview of the fundamental principles to take into account in any feng shui investigation. Chapters 2 and 3 already gave you a glimpse into the self, and Part II is devoted to how feng shui evaluates the relationship between self and the environment.

Although many believe feng shui is about place, the pyramid school of feng shui contends it is about how a person experiences place. I'm sure you know that places can make us feel good. Most of us can close our eyes and recall a cherished spot, a place that is capable of sweeping away all negativity or a place of awesome inspiration. Upon entering such spaces, we can be amazed, dazzled, or inspired, and the moment or a lifetime can be transformed.

Place can also challenge us. Over the last fifteen years a house in my neighborhood has been home to three families that have all suffered divorce, alcoholism, and illness. It is easy to attribute these problems to mysterious phenomena, but rational explanations can be found for many seemingly enigmatic events. Mold can cause irrational behavior as can lack of sunlight. This home is surrounded by large heavily leafed trees, and its windows do not receive direct sunlight. Lack of light might cause depression, thereby causing other difficulties. Sometimes emotional problems can be caused or exacerbated by toxins or other unhealthy conditions in a home. VOCs (volatile organic compounds) are literally exhaled from materials such as glues, rubbers, pressed woods, paints, varnishes, stains, carpets, and fibers. Since this home was prefabricated, it is likely to have many unhealthy materials impregnated with toxic substances that might be leaching into the air.

Human beings react to place on many levels. We are first and foremost biological creatures who have been handed a plate of genetics resulting in our unique as well as common human responses. In addition to biology we are influenced by culture, geography, gender, and generation. The pyramid school has been developed so that feng shui can be applied in any culture, at any time, for any person. This school looks at each person's singularity, including experience, personality, and emotional content, before deciding how he or she may be influenced by place. Place is experienced somewhat differently by each of us; therefore, any place can be either positive or negative, depending on who is perceiving it.

> **Human beings have universal reactions to certain stimuli. In that way we all respond to place similarly.**

Biology is the first layer evaluated in feng shui. The Introduction briefly described ingrained biological responses such as the fight-or-flight instinct that helped our ancestors survive life-threatening dangers and continues to serve us today. Other common human responses include clenching our fists when angry, which prepares us to fight, and wrinkling up our nose when we see or smell something disgusting, which opens a broader passage for odor to be detected and allowed our ancestors to determine whether something might be poisonous or harmful. Studies have shown that children's reacting with disgust to pictures of rats, snakes, or spiders even when they have never seen one face-to-face may be an ingrained human response aimed at self-preservation because those who were cautious always had a better chance of survival. Although feeling terrified by a snake, rat, or spider today might not be as helpful as it once was, it takes thousands and thousands of years to alter a beneficial genetic characteristic. By evolutionary timetables we are probably only a few weeks away from those ancestors who needed to be fearful of snakes and spiders, and so we remain phobic.

Culture is another system that shapes our responses and attitudes.

The next level of feng shui investigation is culture, also touched on earlier in the book. Culture is more difficult for most people to factor in when trying to get to know someone. Where we all have the same biology, we do not emerge from a single culture—a fact that is easy to forget because cultural rules and customs become so deeply ingrained and are so full of complex nuances. Take punctuality for example. We are expected to arrive on time for a doctor's appointment, but the doctor is not necessarily expected to keep his or her schedule accurate. Being late for a business meeting is considered grossly inappropriate, but arriving late for a party is not. These distinctions may seem logical to those of us who have grown up with these conventions, but we forget that everyone we meet may not have learned the same behavior.

Aesthetics are acquired via culture. To interpret ancient Chinese feng shui guidelines in a way that is acceptable today, we need to strip away cultural preferences and reveal the kernel or essence that can be applied to all. In traditional feng shui, crystals are used to change the feeling or energy of a place, but crystals are not necessarily accepted as appropriate Western decor. If we strip away the forms dictated by culture, we get to the universal substance: refracting light, a crystal's unique benefit, is needed to alter the energy of a place. Knowing this, we can use a more familiar Western object such as a cut crystal bowl or a paperweight to change a room's energy. Exactly what object we choose will depend on personal taste, a product of both culture and each person's unique experiences.

In pyramid feng shui, the object is less important than the message it conveys, to others and to you. Feng shui teachings incorporate ways to support personal intention to foster change. Using good luck emblems to symbolize intent, for example, can make it easier to remember and further what it takes to instigate change. A penny, rabbit's foot, or crystal might feel lucky because you believe it to be. Hanging a prayer flag, mounting a mezuzah, and decorating a Christmas tree are actions that cement beliefs. It matters less what the symbol is and more that you believe in it.

Not only is it important to remember when getting to know someone that both biology and culture will dictate choices, but it's crucial to distinguish between the two influences. Cultural preferences are learned: while ingrained, they can be flexible. Biological choices are innate: these are what we are all left with when culture and other layers of influence are stripped away; they tell us what is universally beneficial or detrimental.

Feng shui can uncover how relationships and self-empowerment are affected by place. The next few chapters describe feng shui in depth and how to use it as a tool in selecting a mate or augmenting a present relationship. My system for doing that is based on a technique I call *scope-ing*, introduced in Chapter 5, which analyzes the symbols, color, objects, positioning, and elements in a person's home to perceive a fuller picture of that person's outer and inner selves. Chapter 6 explains how feng shui incorporates into that analysis the Tao, yin and yang, and chi evident in these aspects of a person's home. Chapter 7 explains another tool fundamental to feng shui, the ba-gua, a template you can superimpose over a home or any part of it to see how the occupant's physical world expresses various aspects of his or her emotional life. In Chapter 8 you'll learn how the five elements of feng shui express your personality and emotions. Each of the next five chapters is devoted to one of the elements. You will uncover the elements that define your personality as well as your emotions. Moreover, you will learn what characteristics, both positive and challenging, you will face within yourself or in partnership with another.

5

THE TECHNIQUE
OF SCOPE-ING

*"Objects, like people, come in and out of our
lives and awareness not in some random
meaningless pattern ordained by Fate, but in a
clearly patterned framework that sets the stage
for greater and greater self-understanding."*
Claire Cooper Marcus, *House as
a Mirror of Self*

If you really want to know someone, look at the objects he or
she has chosen to live with. These things are much more revealing
of a person's nature than any conversation can be. In this book I
offer a technique called *scope-ing* by which you can analyze symbols, colors, objects, positioning, and elements to gain a greater
understanding of someone else or yourself. Through scope-ing
you'll see that the furniture, accessories, colors, patterns, and objects
of art in a home that seem like disparate lines actually merge to create a more detailed blueprint of self.

**The symbology of artwork and other
objects expresses parts of ourselves
that are sometimes not easy to see at
first blush of a relationship.**

Symbols

The eminent psychologist E. Prelinger asked a group of people to identify how they viewed themselves by sorting 160 items on a continuum from "self" to "nonself." After the physical body, values, and personal identifying categories such as occupation and age, the participants chose possessions most frequently as a description of self. The choices made when selecting a painting, furniture, carpeting, etc., all seemed to be attached to the notion of how they perceived themselves.

Recently, I did a feng shui consultation at the home of an attractive forty-five-year-old real estate agent who had never married. She expressed to me that at forty-five one of her new goals was to finally settle down with a permanent relationship. Within minutes of my arrival, I discovered a trail of consistent messages revealed by the symbols expressed in her artwork. Most of it consisted of images of solo women, such as a bust of a Native American warrior and a photograph of a woman alone on a beach. I also saw that she had in several locations one solitary comfortable chair. The location of these chairs together with the artwork sent the message that she preferred the autonomy of being alone. These messages did nothing to further her goal of having a lasting intimate alliance.

Symbols can be infused in many ways. Repetitive themes in artwork, collections, or duplications can reveal critical pieces of information. A woman I know reveals that she feels mistreated through her passion for her five greyhounds, which, in my state of Florida, are creatures subjected to questionable treatment by racetracks. Another woman has more than one hundred candles around her home. Having recently overcome a drug and alcohol addiction, she seems to be symbolizing her need for purification. My mother's love of owls in some way expresses her desire to be thought of as intellectual and wise.

Color

Nature and the human body often use the same color to express similar phenomena. Blood, for example, is red, as is fire. The element fire, or its association with warmth, is as vital to the earth as blood is to us. Therefore, it is easy to see why red—as opposed to black, white, yellow, or blue—is associated with an energetic life force.

**A favorite color reflects one's
emotional essence.**

Colors have deep emotional as well as physical properties, and much is revealed by an inclination to use one color repeatedly. Chapter 6 goes into the meaning of color in depth, but for now, know that it is important to note a dominant color theme of each room as well as the overall environment.

Elaine, a massage therapist, painted the walls of her massage therapy room deep green. This, coupled with the dark green carpeting, made the setting different from most massage rooms, which are often light colors. Upon reflection, I realized choosing vivid green represented a deep commitment on Elaine's part to help her clients emerge from the restraints of pain or stress, for green is the color that represents change and growth.

OBJECTS

Objects express our interests and are sometimes used to express deeply felt emotions. A collector of replicas of boats is likely to hunger for some form of freedom, while a coin collector is likely to be happy focused on achieving goals here and now.

Some homes are filled to the brim with objects, and some have almost none. Recently when I was filming a TV show, we visited the home of a woman who had almost no extraneous objects. It could have been a model home except for a few family photographs. Upon querying her about her interests, I learned that she was completely dependent on a partner to fill her life and that, aside from that, very little intrigued her. Another woman, Joan, had a clutter of mugs, glasses, calendars, pottery, oven gloves, refrigerator magnets, prints, bath mats, shower curtains, brooches, earrings, rings, and clothing, all with cats on them. As it turned out, she worked obsessively to save, shelter, and find homes for cats. She had never been married and had no deep personal long-lasting ties. Did her cat decor represent her substitution of cats for human relationships? Or did her message that cats were her passion prevent the development of human intimacies? I don't know, but unless she reduced clutter, change seemed unlikely.

> **The amount and variety of objects around a home often represent what is important to us and how many interests we have.**

POSITIONING

By analyzing positioning we can expose what might be unexpressed. Without warning Marvin left Rebecca. She would not have been shocked had she noticed their home held no visible trace of Marvin's interests. Although he was an avid collector of gadgets, fishing gear, and sports magazines, he stashed them in the garage. Nothing expressing Marvin was in their home's main living spaces. Where we position our valuables, our favorite chair or treasures, can speak volumes about how we feel about other members in a family as well as our place in a family structure.

> **Where we place a desk, a reading chair, or a collection of books can unearth how we feel about ourselves or others.**

ELEMENTS

Albert Einstein spent a great deal of his life searching for a unified theory of the universe, as does contemporary physicist, Stephen Hawking, who theorizes in his book *Black Holes and Baby Universes* that the universe is one huge entity. Both Einstein and Hawking believe there is an overall pattern in which all parts are players. Since we are no different from all systems in the natural world, the five elements (fire, earth, metal, water, and wood) used to describe our physical world can also be used to describe categories of human behavior. Each of the five elements has an implied personality, with the potential for both positive and negative. Although most of us can identify in some way with some attributes of all of the elements, typically we lean toward the personality traits and emotional proclivities of one or two of the five elements. In this way nature and our way of expressing ourselves are unified, as the great minds of our century have suspected.

After I delivered my son, Zachary, my parents came bounding into my hospital room, extolling the familiar virtues of our family. "We knew exactly which one he was even without looking at the names," they cooed. Querying them, I discovered they had correctly chosen the baby, who besides the genetically consistent dark hair and skin our family members have was the one who was kicking and tossing around while looking perfectly content. "Just like his mother!" they exclaimed.

It was true. Zachary was not a surprise addition to a family whose members prided themselves on being outgoing, active, and intense.

Whether or not you have ever observed a room filled with infants and been struck by the inherent differences they already displayed, you probably have noticed the down-to-the-bones differences among people. Felix and Oscar, the stars in that deliciously funny TV show "The Odd Couple," were two diametrically opposite types trying to live together and survive their differences. We are typed by certain proclivities in our genetic structure and interact with our surroundings in ways that individualize us from birth. If circumstances don't force us to change, we usually express similar personality traits throughout life.

> **Our expressed personality as well as our hidden emotions can be detected by the elements we choose to live with.**

You can identify the elements in your own home and use them to initiate positive change, but first you have to understand how the elements are expressed in the physical world. For example, if you are a water person and a potential partner is an earth person, adding fire will prevent the earth partner from feeling enervated because fire ignites earth with energy to counteract the water partner's potential tendency to emotionally saturate an earth person. To gather the appropriate information and initiate change, you need to know which elements are reflected in your own home, providing clues to your own nature. First know yourself, and then do the same for your partner. Only then will you know which other elements will bring the two of you into balance.

The following are some examples of how each element is expressed by shape, line, and color. Knowing these attributes will give you the skills to evaluate a home elementally.

The Five Elements Comprising All Physical Objects

Fire

Shape: triangle, cone

Line: zigzag, crooked

Color: red

Earth

Shape: square

Line: equal, straight, sturdy

Color: terra-cotta (or the color of the soil in your area)

Metal

Shape: circle, arc

Line: curved, ring-shaped, sleek

Color: reflective, white, silver, gold, copper

Water

Shape: amorphous

Line: curved, undulating, wavy

Color: blue, black

Wood

Shape: rectangle

Line: straight, long, striped

Color: green

Every object is made of some form of earth, metal, wood, or a combination of these three of the five elements. Earth objects include pottery, glass, bricks, tiles, sinks, tubs, and dishes. Metal objects include brass, silver, chrome, steel, pewter, bronze, and gold as well as all plastics, resins, polymers, cellulose, and glues. Wood objects include any items made from plants, including the material wood (not the color of wood), rubbers, and natural fibers.

While all objects are made of earth, metal, or wood, they are all formed by either fire or water. For example, a papier-mâché sculpture is wood/water, and a carved sculpture is wood/fire. Some examples of how elements and the catalysts water and fire are joined:

Fire/fire—oven, fireplace, sauna
Fire/water—radiators

Earth/fire—porcelain or stoneware, clay sculpture, bricks
Earth/water—soil, terraria, glass

Metal/fire—steel tables, chrome frames, appliances, wiring,
    computers
Metal/water—soft plastics, varnishes, shiny floor coverings,
    synthetic carpets and fabrics, mirrors, paints

Water/fire—steam room
Water/water—fountains, fish tanks, sinks, tubs (when in use)

Wood/fire—carved sculpture or furniture, plank floors, wood-
    block prints
Wood/water—paper, bentwood furniture, cardboard furniture,
    lithographs, canvas for paintings

INDIVIDUALS' NICHES OF GESTALT

Each human being carves out a niche in the cosmos that expresses him or her uniquely in place and time. One's choices, when factored together, have a completeness—a gestalt—that reflects that person's uniqueness. We all have, to some degree, a style. The style may be to have no obvious style at all or may be identified with a period of time, a socioeconomic group, or an aesthetic point of view. What is chosen makes an important statement.

Can we infer that one who chooses antiques will be more likely to defend traditional values than one who selects modern furnishings? If the contents of a home clearly cost more than a person's livelihood could support, should we assume that the person's sense of self-worth needs bolstering by material possessions? Does aligning with a particular art form make one feel stylish? Scope-ing will teach you to pay attention to things otherwise missed and can help—when supported by behavior and actions—to illuminate a person's true nature and answer such questions.

Naturally, choices made in any environment might have arisen from an obligation to the past. Have you ever purchased an article of clothing that you thought you should own? I certainly have. These selections are likely to become the stuff of garage sales or consignment shops. If you observe something out of sync in an environment, it might be there for the same reason that you purchased a wild hat or conservative slacks. Look for consistency of selections; the exceptions are often just that.

We all conjoin with other human beings, in either harmonious or treacherous combinations, and it's up to us to know how to adapt and attune ourselves within the framework of who we really are. Using scope-ing as a discriminating tool to assist us in understanding another's nature as well as our own can help us transcend future problems.

6

TAO, YIN AND YANG, AND CHI

"The scientist's religious feelings take the form of a rapturous amazement at the harmony of natural law, which reveals an intelligence of such superiority that, in comparison with it, all the systematic thinking of human beings is an utterly insignificant reflection."
Albert Einstein

Science and philosophy, whose paths over the millennium have seemed divergent, are on a collision course. Today's best scientific minds are discovering the philosophy in science and the science in philosophy. Groups come together in prayer to effect biological changes, and science now knows that the way we choose to look at something determines how we see it. The difference, it seems, is that philosophers speak in words and scientists speak in mathematics.

Understanding the marriage of philosophy and science is imperative to accepting the efficacy of examining an environment to learn about the people who have designed it. Grasping how each human being is intertwined with all of life is so fundamental that to ignore it would be like a dietitian suggesting you ingest only one food group. The Tao, yin/yang, and chi are the philosophical underpinnings of feng shui and represent some of the basic similarities between science and philosophy.

Tao—Connections

Tao is a concept that expresses the way all things are connected to each other. We are linked profoundly to all things, and not even the smallest particle of matter is insignificant to the largest scheme. The Tao is neither an object nor a process, yet it represents how everything functions. A home can represent the essence of Tao when it supports all natural processes, connects to the community, functions with grace for its inhabitants, supports each individual with consistency, and stimulates all parts to thrive, not just survive. Balance in all things is essential to the Tao.

Cultures search for a model to represent the Tao, be it a god-like form or a scientific law. Albert Einstein's desire to find a unified theory of the universe is not too far removed from Buddha, Jesus, and Muhammad's quest to reveal the meaning of life. These great thinkers sought to uncover fundamental truths. How our lives are interwoven and what are the best models to live by are some of the answers revealed by an understanding of the way things are, or Tao. To be appropriately in the moment, in our lives, and in this world and to honor what exists is the essence of Tao.

> **The Tao is the way we are linked to all things.**

What would happen if you didn't have one spot to keep paper and pencils? Each time you wanted to write a note you would be challenged to reconstruct the last time you wrote so you could locate these implements. To be in the Tao implies a pattern that incorporates both the simplest and most efficient functioning. Keeping paper and pencils near a phone, in a desk drawer, by your bed, or where you are likely to be inspired to write would serve the Tao better than having to retrieve these items from a place not typically used or inspirational for writing.

The Tao is unknowable and indescribable, and like the wind it cannot be seen. We must judge the Tao by its effect on other things. Rather than knowing the Tao, it is better to understand how we are enmeshed in it. The pertinent question, it seems, is not what the universe is, but rather what part of it we are and how we affect the whole. Stephen Hawking suggested in *Black Holes and Baby Universes* that we may be no more than a dot or quantum in a gargantuan organism called the universe. Yet in our immediate world we have the potential to be sensitive, connected, and important to the whole as was the Dutch boy who crammed his tiny finger into a leaking dike and saved a city. Thus, in each moment, our potential to rescue the universe and ourselves is significant.

We can, when viewing another's abode, observe the Tao of space as well as its individual parts. It is possible to see how each part fits into a picture that is as complete and finite as a painting. Each portion helps us discern the entire picture. Observing an individual's choices reveals the unarticulated.

Even as objects reveal other parts of a person, they cannot, of course, exactly replicate the complexity of the subconscious. Therefore, the Tao or overall story is disclosed only through direct contact with the creator as well as his or her choices.

Connections Express the Tao

The word *connection* can serve as a key to evaluating a home's Tao. Ultimately all things work best when they are unfolded appropriately. My idea of a good morning, for example, is connected directly to the previous night's sleep, what's happening in my life, and the weather outside. Even a Lamborghini wouldn't function optimally if there were no fuel in the gas tank, no driver, and the road it was traveling on was filled with ice and snow. We are connected to the conditions around us, and to understand what optimal functioning is, you need to examine all parts. When something is jarring, overused, deficient, or inappropriate for its setting, maximum functioning is impaired.

> **To experience the Tao, observe the whole and then consider how the individual parts fit in.**

Signs of Being Out of the Tao

Clutter

Where there is clutter, there are roadblocks. Since the Tao can be described as "the way," when there is clutter "the way" is blocked.

Often clutter can pinpoint challenging areas of a person's life as was the case for my college roommate who suffered from depression and finally sought psychiatric help. Her therapist, upon learning that her closet was stuffed as full as a trash container after a rock concert, suggested she tackle cleaning up this mess. She would, her therapist implied, be ready to look at her problems once the clutter was removed. A television network executive who had documents piled way too high on her desk rose to the top position in her department when she followed my suggestion to pare down the stack to a manageable size. Even when a person appears to be functioning optimally, removing or organizing clutter invariably produces benefits.

> **The location of clutter pinpoints problem areas of life.**

The absence of disorder empowers us. I feel on top of the world when I come downstairs each morning and am greeted by a pristine kitchen. The few times I don't clean up after dinner, I find myself cranky and less enthusiastic about beginning the day. By locating areas of clutter, you can come to some general conclusions about a person. The location of clutter reveals the content of a person's inner struggle.

Location of Clutter	Could Indicate . . .
entrance of a home	fear of relationships
inside a closet	unwilling to examine emotions
in a kitchen	resenting or overwhelmed by caretaking
next to a bed	desire for change or escape
on a desk	frustration, fear of letting go, or need for control
in a corner behind a door	detachment from others
under a piece of furniture	importance of appearances
in a cellar	procrastination
in an attic	living in the past
in a garage	inability to actualize
all over	anger and self-loathing

No Pets or Plants or Living Objects Requiring Care

Especially when there are no children in a home, pets or plants indicate a willingness to be responsible for and accepting of others' needs. Moreover, when we bring living creatures or organisms inside our homes, we are metaphorically stepping outside our personal shell into the Tao or bigger picture. Honoring the processes involved with nurturing life can parallel the way we treat ourselves and others.

No matter how busy a schedule is, an adult who never cooks or who doesn't offer a snack or a drink to visitors probably is low on empathy. The ease with which we connect to caring or nurturing is often expressed in how we entertain, cook, or serve others.

Caring for living things is essential to the Tao.

No Photographs of Family or Friends

Be cautious when attaching yourself to someone who has severed relationships with past family members or friends, because the ability to divorce oneself from the past might rear its destructive head with you. Having a history of relationships is a sure sign of being able to sustain present relationships or develop new ones. Unless past relationships were seriously destructive, the ability to forgive and learn is essential to fulfilling present enmeshments. Photographs or cherished objects representing relationships are a sign of the ability and desire to connect in sustained, meaningful ways.

Displaying photographs of only deceased family members implies a disconnection in the present. Moreover, photographs relating only to the past indicate a fixation on what has been more than what can be. The best combination by far is a mix of past and present, representing revering the past while still being rooted in the here and now.

Displaying past and present connections to family and friends is appropriate in the Tao of time.

Few or No Accessories

Accessories are items we have in our home for no other purpose than to delight us. Accessories satisfy us as they reveal us. Choosing to purchase a mattress tells us little about a person's uniqueness in the way a painting or artifact informs us. I have been inside homes of the rich and poor that have been bereft of objects. Lack of accessories often exposes a disinclination to expose ourselves freely and openly to others.

No Books

Books as opposed to newspapers or magazines are lasting images of values, interests, and tastes. When a home is devoid of books, we are at a loss to determine important connections. Reading helps us savor values and concepts and stretches us to keep refining beliefs.

Routines

Routines weave the threads of each day into a larger tapestry. However, routines, like anything else, can get out of hand. When does a routine become an obsession rather than a guide? When it becomes more important than the act itself, such as when the precise placement of a vase or a bowl creates more satisfaction than the viewing of it. If you visit a friend who puffs up the pillows as soon as you stand up, or have a boss who rearranges the chair the moment you leave it, or a date who habitually refolds the dinner napkin prior to leaving a restaurant, you are experiencing the dark side of routines.

When I was growing up, my parents had an unbending rule. Not only did the family have dinner together every night, but dinner was served precisely at 6:00 P.M. Pity any one of us who did not show up at this precise hour. Unfortunately, I had a desire with which my parents did not agree. I wanted to see the New York City Easter Parade in person.

And so it came to pass that on the Easter Sunday in my thirteenth year a girlfriend and I ventured into New York City. Our real intentions eluded detection because we left home with tennis rackets in hand. Overwhelmed by a sense of adventure, we didn't notice that the bus ride took two hours instead of its normal one. By the time we finished ogling at the variety and oddity of headgear and returned for the trip home, it was way past 6:00 P.M. Feeling like

Cinderella, who panicked when she realized she had stayed far too long at the ball, I was gripped by fear, for I had missed a sacred family routine. The only reasonable excuse for this sin, I reasoned, was kidnapping. Stoically, I phoned home with the news. Assuring my parents we were unharmed and had eluded the kidnappers by our quick actions, we returned home by bus to meet our fate.

Routines can reveal appropriate or dysfunctional behavior.

Needless to say, both sets of parents met us at the bus stop. My friend's parents had tears in their eyes; mine seethed with suspicion. We were separated and each taken home for further questioning. I held fast to the story, but in no time at all we received a telephone call from my friend's parents informing my parents of the truth. Unlike me, she had not broken a sacred routine and evidently had had an easier time confessing. Such compulsory routines often have deleterious effects on life.

Routines can disconnect us. Sometimes they are established to camouflage fears or lack of control or to display a false image to the world. It is up to you to determine whether any routine seems extreme or normal or if it has a positive or negative impact on the observed life. A broken routine that makes one feel slightly panicked, angry, or upset when interrupted is often one that disconnects from the normal rhythms of life. Those rhythms require some flexibility if we are to be undaunted by diversity.

Signs of Troublesome Routines

having only certain items on a refrigerator shelf

having an unchangeable fixed time for dining

cleaning compulsively

having to keep a certain door (bathrooms and closets excluded) open or shut all the time

having to let a telephone ring a particular number of times before picking it up

having to pull a window shade down to an exact position or open curtains precisely to a marked spot

Lack of Past Connections

Bart met Annabelle through a personal ad. Both couldn't believe their luck in meeting someone bright, articulate, and adult, and they mutually pursued each other. They both loved music and films and had a zest for travel. Their differences, however, could be seen clearly in their respective homes.

By her midforties Annabelle has accumulated two pets and a home filled with plants and artwork and a host of comfortable, well-cared-for furnishings. Bart, however, although the same age, had arrived recently in his town with nothing more than what he carried in the trunk of his car. His rental apartment was sparse, and he added nothing to it to personalize it. He ate his meals from Styrofoam containers and had no memorabilia of past family or friends. They married, but when Bart's problems—his inability to be connected to friends or a job—could no longer be overlooked, they parted painfully. Had Annabelle understood the obvious signs of disconnection in Bart's home, she could have avoided a tragic mistake.

The Tao is all-inclusive, and when parts are ignored we pay the price somewhere down the road. Like the strains of a well-crafted song, the Tao of personal space has notes that when played should produce a melodious refrain.

YIN AND YANG

All things strive for balance. When imbalance exists in nature, it ultimately is reversed. Sunshine follows darkness, and dying follows birth; all things have counterbalances. If water did not put out fire or if earth did not absorb water, we would perish in a raging inferno or be swept away. Balance creates equanimity and imbalance turmoil.

In the simplest form yin and yang are opposites linked together in an unbroken chain. When one extreme is reached, a condition flips to the other. For example, if you were scorched with a piece of dry ice, you might think you were burned. One side of a spectrum often feels like its opposite.

The physical body and the human spirit tend to seek balance or homeostasis. After we are enraged, we often fall asleep with exhaustion. A period of depression can be followed by euphoria. Know that extremes are often not stable, and once the extreme or peak is reached the flip side is likely to follow.

Yin and yang are opposites but not adversarial; they represent the extremes necessary to support life.

However, all of us have times when we experience imbalance. This is part of the sea of life with its waves that ceaselessly roll in and out. The song "I've Grown Accustomed to Her Face" includes the words "I've grown accustomed to her . . . smiles, her frowns, her ups, her downs . . . like breathing out and breathing in." To be in harmony is to understand and be comfortable with each other's extremes. Recognizing and understanding how to be in harmony with another's extremes is part of what it takes to construct a healthy relationship.

Unlike our Western notion of opposites, yin and yang represent extremes that complete a positive cycle. Whatever the context is, there are always extremes. Even prisoners of war had to find joy along with sorrow, friendship along with hate, or their survival would have been at risk. Without the ability to embrace contrasts, life would be difficult if not just boring.

Unfortunately yin and yang have been misunderstood in the West. Yin, we are told, represents female and is connected with cold, wet, dark, death, and quiet. This depiction seems depressing, especially for women. The more sought-after yang traits of warm, dry, alive, and active that are associated with male, in the traditional interpretation could lead to the conclusion that yin is bad and yang is good. Not so. They need each other, or the contrast would not be perceived. It is better to think of yin and yang as points on a continuous circle, each one leading back to the other. Better to think of yin as breathing in or turning inward and yang as breathing out or being extroverted.

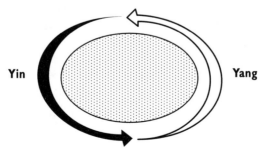

Yin is like breathing in, and yang is like breathing out.

Complete balance is a sought-after state in all of nature. Being in balance means having a little bit of everything. An interior space saturated with one color, element, or line is not balanced and over time can cause those in this space to become unbalanced. A good example is today's typical office, with too many metal elements— metal furnishings, few windows with a nature view, too many electrical gadgets, and few colors other than white, gray, or beige. The metal element promotes mental but not emotional or physical activities. Too much metal element causes office workers to experience mental fatigue, emotional inactivity, and a feeling of displacement or disconnection.

Balance includes a range of experiences with an emphasis on elements necessary to complement those living in the space. For example, an excitable person who is easily overstimulated would not want too many fire elements in an environment. The calming influence of serene water or the bracing supports of earth would be better suited to balance a person who has a fiery nature.

Positive Yin and Yang

Yin	Yang
dark/resting	light/active
cold/turning inward or thinking	hot/expressing and communicating
empty/ready to receive	full/ready to give
curved lines/deliberate	straight lines/ready to take action
soft/compassionate	hard/exacting
low/willing to follow	high/desiring to lead
quiet/open to learning	noisy/open to teaching

My uncle Hy, a sculptor, always wanted a home with only one room filled with a few treasured pieces of furniture and decorated mostly with art and books. The colors he loved were deep purples and blacks, and the lines of fabrics and his own sculptures were undulating and relaxed. Filled with quiet music, plush area rugs, and upholstered chairs, his dream home would be the quintessential yin. He held on to this vision of a home all his life, and the image was consistent with who he was. He was the relative who was always interested in what we children were doing and thinking. His imagined and real yin homes expressed much of his internal nature. He was more interested in breathing in another's essence than impressing us with his.

The quality of either yin or yang has the potential to be beneficial or harmful. Not all yin atmospheres are positive as was my uncle's. The following chart delineates the negative extremes of yin and yang.

Challenging Yin and Yang

Yin	Yang
dark/immobile	light/frenzied
cold/closed off	hot/compulsive
empty/drawing life force from others	full/unable to listen
curved lines/can't make change	straight lines/won't stay the course
soft/victim	hard/perpetrator
low/shy	high/controlling
quiet/displaying a false image	noisy/trying to enhance lack of self-esteem

A childhood friend's home had a strange assortment of furnishings in the living room. Only hard chairs without upholstery were available for seating. Until that time, I had never seen a living room without either a sofa or cushioned chairs. My friend's parents were demanding, exacting people who were not affectionate or terribly supportive of their four sons. Their stoicism seemed to me heartless and exacting, just like the seating. Their living room was way too yang.

Another friend, who wants nothing more than to become a full-time writer, has nothing in her office that is not cushioned. All the seating is so soft and yielding that it's hard to get up because the cushions surround you and practically hold you in place. I feel lazy in her office, as I suspect she does too. It is easy to see why she has not been able to motivate herself to become successful as a writer. This room is too yin and doesn't provide the springboard from which she can catapult her ideas into orbit.

All things strive for balance. When we retain conditions that leave us in a state of imbalance, we are creating a more stressful lifestyle. Whether that stress is masking something too painful to deal with or simply a vestige of the past, it is best to identify imbalances and discern how to deal with them so they won't become formidable barriers.

On the other hand, don't be afraid to create some imbalance. It might be just the right catalyst for change. Sometimes extremes can be helpful. When I was first separated from my husband, I felt strangely compelled to run out and buy the fluffiest comforters I could find to cover my bed. Although I am not the type to languish in bed, I did find this extravagance soothing in light of the recent reduction in the availability of warmth. Piling my bed high with comforters might seem strange, but when viewed in the light of the moment, it was a wise device to assuage a painful time in my life.

Yin and yang are opportunities as well as actualities. With a full spectrum of experiences we are likely to feel more alive. Understanding how yin and yang can be expressed will aid us in managing life's experiences.

How Yin and Yang Are Expressed

Yin	Yang
dark	bright
cool	warm
curved lines	straight lines
undefined patterns	defined patterns
heavily scented	fresh air
confined	open
cluttered	sparse
stillness	movement

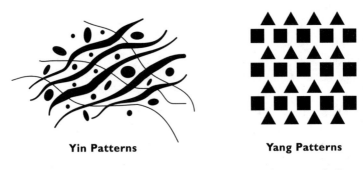

Yin Patterns   **Yang Patterns**

Yin patterns have curved lines, and yang patterns have straight lines.

CHI

CHI

Life is intimately connected to chi, which can be described by the words *energy* or *vitality*. Chi is the spirit of a person, a place, and the intangible communication system of all things. We fall in love with people because of their chi, and when we list a lover's attributes, we typically enumerate the chi attributes or those that express a discernable vitality. We are more likely to say someone is kind, generous, smart, or a good tennis player than to say he prefers green, eats salads daily, or likes to solve complex puzzles. Nothing exists that does not exude some form of energy or chi.

The word *chi* has been misunderstood and used to describe things imprecisely. It is used to describe something amorphous—without definition or form. I hear people making statements like "Chi is sucked out of a room with a window across from an entrance door" or "The chi can't circulate in this house." These descriptions are meaningless and confusing because they do not pinpoint the sensory experience that is lacking when there is a problem with chi.

Chi describes a sensory experience—what we see, smell, feel, and hear.

Do we look at the scene outside if a window is positioned across from an entrance door? Are the colors too dark in a room, is the lighting too low, or is there too much furniture to permit us to move freely inside a home? Our vitality is affected by seeing, hearing, smelling, and touching. Chi should be described as it affects one of the senses.

Chi, like preferences, takes many forms. A rock sits stoically in or on the earth. It moves only when propelled by an outside force. While a rock's shape is altered over time, to us it appears unchanging. On the other hand, a dandelion appears one day out of nowhere, unveils a yellow blossom that metamorphoses into a ragged dustball of ethereal white, only to dissipate easily by air movement or a passerby's touch. Both forms of chi appear different to us. One seems unyielding and the other fleeting.

Because of the size difference, a small pebble acts differently than a boulder in a rushing stream. A dandelion having the bad luck to take root on a lawn that is mowed daily reacts differently from one that can grow uninterrupted. In short, the chi varies because of an endless series of combinations, situations, and experiences. When scope-ing another's space, you will find that the very same print, object, or rug will disperse different chi depending on the setting.

Chi is the reaction by our senses to conditions in the physical world. To determine if chi is positive or not, you must describe the sensor it is filtered through. There is sight chi, which includes color, line, and material; movement chi; sound chi; scent chi; and chi experienced by touching. Only when chi is defined can it be analyzed. Here's an example of movement chi. The chi of a long, straight pathway makes a person walk faster than if the pathway were shorter or curved. In a train station a long, straight pathway makes crowds rush ahead even more hastily than they would normally. Curving or shortening this path would slow down rushing chi. Sight chi is illustrated by the following example. The eye tends to look at the long view when one is walking down a long, narrow hall rather than taking in more peripheral information. Think about how one tends not to look at paintings hung on the walls of long, straight hallways. The chi of sight is distracted from the immediate surroundings toward the final goal (the end of the hallway).

Because much of what we experience is rooted to the biological system that helped our species survive, our reactions to stimuli are often alike. Most of us feel stymied by having a wall positioned too closely in front of us when entering a home. It stops our natural tendency to move forward. A window positioned across from an entrance to a room attracts our eye because the eye naturally moves to the direction of light.

Because these responses are inborn, chi, like love at first sight, is immediate and overwhelming and consumes us without giving us time to cogitate or rationalize. The experience of the chi is internalized without effort; we can't help sensing and responding to another's chi or energy. Recall your first day at high school or anytime where you met a large group of people for the first time. Without knowing why, you reacted to another's chi and either liked him or her or not. If you could remember that exact moment, you could dissect why you felt akin to that person: the way he or she smiled at you, a whiff of talcum powder that you liked, the melodic tone in the person's voice, or the feel of the person's arm around your shoulder.

How does chi express itself in a home? In the simplest way, vivid colors, large objects, or too much furniture express active chi, while blank walls or few accessories express little chi. One is not better than the other, and it is important to realize that all things can be supporting or challenging depending on who you are and what needs manifest in your life. To read a home's chi and determine its message, consider all senses.

Sight

 Most information is taken in with our eyes. Westerners pay less attention to other sensory experiences and take in information mainly by looking. Color, line, material, overall shape, and meaning are to be considered when observing objects.

The natural world and the human body use equivalent colors for similar roles. For example, the sun is experienced as yellow. It is also the color of the cells in our eyes that allow us to see clearly. In fact, when these cells deteriorate, we lose our visual acuity in the same way as all sighted creatures see less clearly when the sun goes down. The color yellow represents clarity in both the sun and our eyes.

In addition to a color's general use, personal experience determines if we respond positively or negatively to a color. An unpleasant association with a color can affect how we feel about it for a lifetime. One day I was wearing a fluffy pink angora collar over a plain pink wool cardigan and a pink and black felt skirt (yes, with a poodle sewn on it) during a junior high cooking class. We were preparing a baked dish, and I was assigned to light the gas stove. I suppose I waited just a little too long between turning on the gas and bringing a lit match toward the gas jet's opening. A whoosh and a bang bellowed from the belly of the oven before I could completely remove my head. Most of my bangs and eyebrows were gone, and to this day I cringe when I look at pink clothing because I blamed my bad luck on wearing all pink.

When certain colors become popular, they typically relate closely to the issues that are in the forefront at that time. For example, today the color orange is more popular than it has been for decades. Orange is the color of fusion and implies an interest in the good of all over the interest of the few. The "me" generation seems to have had its last hurrah, and the popularity of the color orange represents a new direction.

The Chi of Color

It's not by accident that we choose to live with certain colors. Whether we know it or not, often the choice of a color can, on the positive side, supply us with emotional benefits or, conversely, sustain our problems. For example, if a person is stuck in an old habit and can't seem to change, having a lot of earth colors could be detrimental to altering it. Earth colors supply us with the satisfaction of stability and support appreciating the here and now rather than the desire for change. Therefore when scope-ing one's own or another's space, know that a color, while expressing parts of a person, can indicate either a benefit or a detriment to their life.

Red

Red invokes a strong life force. Our blood, the conductor of vitality throughout the body, perfectly represents the spirit of red. All colors emit waves or vibrations, and red has the longest wavelength of all colors. It fills our visual field like a giant flag waving in the midst of smaller ones. You can't help seeing red first. Many flowers, which depend on being seen by birds, bees, and butterflies to pollinate their species, are red. Red is a lifeline to existence, a display of animation and activity. Using red implies the desire to be noticed, invested, and important. No wonder the robes of religious leaders are often red.

What Choosing Red May Mean

Positive	Challenging
vital	self-centered
animated	inflated self-worth
active	domineering

Yellow

Brightness, cheer, and clarity are associated with yellow. Choosing yellow implies a desire to be clear, to observe, and to be observed. The flip side of yellow signals one should pay attention, for yellow represents a source needing detoxification, purification, or regeneration. The color yellow is associated with aging and loss, such as fall leaves on their way to extinction and the color of faded paper as it deteriorates.

What Choosing Yellow May Mean

Positive	Challenging
cheerful	tired
observant	declining
optimistic	forcing congeniality

Blue

Gazing at a blue surface makes us feel less overwhelmed. When wishing for or seeking answers to life's unsolved riddles, the inclination is to peer upward at the sky or down into a deep pool of water. Seeking guidance, turning inward, stilling our minds, and calming our emotions are often associated with a blue sky or blue water.

Faber Birren, a respected color researcher, unveiled studies showing that when spending time in an all-blue room a subject's blood pressure and breathing rate were actually lowered. Blue calms us and allows us to slow down. Visualizing a blue room is a good way to begin a meditation.

Those who choose blue as a room's primary color can be articulating either the need to be still or the need to self-aggrandize. While we become calm seeing blue, we also lose a connection with others and turn inward, focusing on our own needs and dreams. Blue reinforces the belief in self and can be associated with either self-confidence or egocentricity.

What Choosing Blue May Mean

Positive	Challenging
self-confident	egocentric
supportive	self-absorbed
relaxed	aloof
able to yield	apathetic

Green

Green is the color of photosynthesis. The process of growth is the central meaning of the color green; therefore green inspires us to learn, develop, and change.

Green is also associated, in some ways incorrectly, with relaxation because we associate green with nature. However, the color of plants is only one of many sensory experiences engaged outdoors. The music of birds often punctuates the stillness, a cool breeze can brush across our skin, and often a delicious scent fills the air. It is the combination of experiences that soothes, restores, and refreshes, not just seeing the color green. Painting a wall green does not duplicate the multisensorial experiences of nature, nor does it calm.

At winter's solstice, we bring in greenery to remind us of the rejuvenation that awaits us in spring. Green offers growth and change and is often the choice of those who are undaunted by the unknown and unafraid of transformation.

What Choosing Green May Mean

Positive	Challenging
adventurous	too scattered
leader	unable to focus
tackles problems well	tending to begin another project before finishing the one before

Orange

Orange is blue's complementary color, which means it is placed opposite blue on the color wheel. It also suggests the opposite meaning. While blue turns one inward, orange fuses one to an ideology outside of or bigger than self. Orange is the choice of Buddhist monks who seek fulfillment by divorcing themselves from personal desires. No wonder orange is not the color chosen for the robes of Catholic priests, who are divined to personally interpret religious principles for the masses. Wearing orange would not serve their authoritarian status. Those who choose orange for a home may be communicating a commitment to a larger process or at least acknowledging the reduced importance of self.

What Choosing Orange May Mean

Positive	Challenging
able to commit	unable to generate ideas
selfless	goalless
charitable	self-satisfied

Purple

Since ultraviolet light is not seen in the visible spectrum, colors that reflect its hue, like violets, purples, and magentas, are often associated with that which is not seen or is not present. Higher consciousness and spirituality are the areas of association. Just as royal purple suggests a position that is not within the boundaries of ordinary folk, those who choose purple for their homes may wish to be outside these common definitions.

Choosing purple for one's environment suggests a desire to be connected with that which has yet to unfold. Teenage girls and those striving to find themselves often have an affinity for this color. It is interesting to note that when people in this group are actualized or grown up, their attraction toward purple dissipates. When you meet an adult whose home is decorated with purple, know that you are likely with someone who has yet to feel completely evolved.

What Choosing Purple May Mean

Positive	Challenging
nonmaterialistic	wanting to be perceived as having a deep spiritual life
seeking a higher purpose	in transition
wants to be noticed	doesn't feel actualized

Black

Black absorbs all light. It suggests that all things are possible; it implies rather than is. Black expresses on some level the paradoxical quality of life. Often I wear black knowing full well that I cannot remain pristine for the duration of an evening. Black will give me the appearance rather than the reality of being clean. In the same way a woman in black exudes mystery, a black room demands that we feel intrigued.

Black is visually experienced as a hole. A black door disappears, as do ten pounds of flesh when I wear a black dress. In fact, black can prevent Alzheimer's patients from escaping their home. Since Alzheimer's patients have ceased to be able to discriminate accurately, they see black as a hole rather than an object. If a black rubber mat is cut into a circle large enough to fill the space in front of an exit door, an Alzheimer's patient will not step on the black area to open a door. Not worrying about a patient escaping while in the bathroom or kitchen can relieve a great deal of pressure on the caretaker.

Rooms with black as a theme imply a desire to astound and puzzle rather than support and assist.

What Choosing Black May Mean

Positive	Challenging
desires to be challenged	feels insecure about choices
not fearful	refuels through others' energy
courageous	negativity can override optimism
bold	concealing something

White

The challenge of being in a white room is not unlike wearing a white outfit. The task is to stay clean and not to compromise its pristine quality. White reflects all and in doing so reveals all. In a white room there is nowhere to hide. Choosing white suggests not wanting to kick back, be easygoing or anonymous.

What Choosing White May Mean

Positive	Challenging
fearless	demands attention
undaunted	too obliging
truthful	lacking strong commitments

The Chi of Line/Shape

A shape is defined by its edges. We sense the heady vitality of the Rocky Mountains from their triangular peaks and the more tractable, approachable Appalachian Mountains via their less aggressive, rounded tops. Lines exude messages just as colors do. Whatever we choose has a line, and by selecting it we have subconsciously chosen a message. Understanding what a shape or form expresses helps put another piece of chi's puzzle into perspective. After color, line and form are to be examined when scope-ing an environment.

Triangles

 Whether it is the agitation of a flame or the dynamics of peaked mountains, a triangular shape is compelling, precarious, and mutable. Over the years I have observed that flame-stick patterns and other triangular designs are used least. When present in fabric, accessories, or furniture's shape, the triangle stirs up a strong reaction. Like a flickering flame, triangles can make us feel insecure, ignite us to action, and deter us from contemplation.

What Choosing a Triangle May Mean

Positive	Challenging
in transition	elusive
energetic	unstable
engaging	accumulates stress

Squares

 With all sides equal, a square is a shape that cannot be toppled easily. Associated with earth and the feeling of being grounded, a square exudes steadfastness, tenacity, and perseverance. When you need change or have a difficult time conjuring up motivation, don't use a square shape. Conversely, when life has been topsy-turvy and you feel pulled in all directions, a square could be the perfect remedy.

What Choosing a Square May Mean

Positive	Challenging
steadfast	clinging
grounded	stuck
tenacious	stubborn

Circles

 The memory of spinning around on a merry-go-round may evoke a vision of blurred faces and the wind splashing cool air on an excited face. Whether rotating actually or visually, the form of a circle lends itself to movement. Look at the outer edge of a circle and notice how your eyes keep moving. With no break or edge, there is little reason for the eyes to stop moving. If you want to give yourself a jump start in the morning, have a circle in view. A circle is a visual cup of coffee.

While the eye is encouraged to keep moving, it is not allowed to wander. There are no lines radiating away from this shape. For that reason a circle is contained and inhibits drifting. In this way a circle contains us and forces us to be in control.

What Choosing a Circle May Mean

Positive	Challenging
mentally active	demanding of precision
accepting of constraints	harassing
investigative	has difficulty putting ideas into action

Undulating or Wavy Shapes

 No matter how long it takes, water seeks and reaches the lowest ground. The Grand Canyon is a spectacular example of water's persistence. Surface watercourses tend to undulate unless bedrock underneath constrains them. People who have no trouble going with the flow or adjusting to any situation are often most comfortable with free-flowing lines. Undulating shapes discourage focus and may encourage daydreaming. If one is inclined to be indecisive, a curved water line may not be a good choice.

What Choosing Undulating or Wavy Lines May Mean

Positive	Challenging
accepting	indecisive
yielding	temperamental
sympathetic	victimized

Rectangles

The tendency for all living things to grow upward or outward while maturing is represented by a vertical or horizontal rectangle. Just as a mighty oak starts out as a twig, the sense of enlargement and movement is associated with the thrust of the rectangle. Stripes and rectangles mimic expansion. Choosing a rectangular pattern for a wallpaper or fabric may indicate comfort with change or a desire for change to occur. In any case, it is a strong shape to select and is not easy to ignore visually.

What Choosing a Rectangle May Mean

Positive	Challenging
willing to change	not wanting permanence
likes challenges	can be erratic
energetic	unpredictable

The Chi of Movement

You may have read in numerous feng shui articles about chi being stuck or moving too quickly. Does this make you wonder if chi has legs or circulates unseen like a tornado? Actually, the movement of chi refers to how *you* move through space, whether by physically transporting your body or having your different sensory receptors engaged.

Referring back to the window across from an entrance door, does it compel you to look at the outside scene? Do you feel guided by the sights or left to drift at your own pace into the scene? Do you feel stymied from walking into the space or compelled to take a path that is uncomfortable or arduous? How we are thwarted or encouraged to move through a space is worthy of note, for the implications can be profound. My friend Joanne placed a baker's rack filled with family photos to the left of her kitchen door. Because her main gathering area was to the right of the kitchen, her guests rarely drifted over to the rack to view the family photos. Placing something important out of the normal areas traversed making it more difficult to view implies a desire to keep that which is out of the normal flow private. When a photo of me makes it to Joanne's baker's rack, I will know I am considered part of the family.

More obvious examples are seen in homes in which it feels arduous to wend one's way amid the furniture to sit down or in which a dining chair is too close to the wall to make it comfortable to sit in. Take note which areas are easy to access and which are not. The very least you will uncover is what is considered private and not easily shared.

What Encourages Movement

Before physically moving through space, we search for a convenient path. If there is no discernible path or one is filled with obstacles, we feel defeated even before entering. When there is insufficient light, an object blocking a full view, or something diverting our attention, we normally circumvent an area.

What Dim Lighting or Obstructions May Indicate

emotional barriers to relationships
frailty of self-esteem
shyness
avoidance of being in the here and now

Chi of Open Space

Years ago while visiting a Frank Lloyd Wright home I was intimidated from going into the main gathering space because of the huge amount of open area between where I entered and the room's furniture. Stripped of supports, I would have had to cover what seemed like miles of highly polished floor to reach a seat. It may be hard to describe exactly, but one instantly recognizes the difference between a room that feels too empty and one that is not.

I once met a man who at forty-eight had only the basic necessities at home. Although he had recently moved into the area, he had no objects that were connected to his past life. Although his hard luck story sounded plausible and his disinterest in material possessions commendable, a red flag was waving in my face. How could someone who was connected to his emotional life have no current reminders—no photographs of his children, no favorite clock, paperweight, or artifact from a vacation? Years later, I discovered that he had a checkered past, one that kept him running away from situations and people. Never was there a place or person who became integrated into his life. He fled each place and divested himself of all persons he had known while there. The vitality or chi of his past was excised from his life as one would remove a malignant tumor. The chi of empty spaces may imply the following.

What Too-Empty Space May Indicate

unable to sustain relationships
emotionally aloof
unable to commit
guarded

SOUND

When we seal ourselves inside to create a soundless landscape, we are shutting ourselves off from life. Even in a desert, the wind rubs together the grains of sand, adding a delicate cadence to a quiet scene. In nature there is rarely complete silence. Sound is not only music and certainly not just voices or electronic devices. A living space needs to include many different sounds. Wind or whirling fans blowing on leaves or lightweight objects rustling when brushed, footsteps on different surfaces, or sound-producing objects like bells are ways to increase auditory stimulation indoors.

Sound may be the most difficult chi to access because when guests are expected most likely a television will be turned off and a stereo turned on. Therefore, noticing the positions of items that produce sound may be more telling than the sound itself. For example, to know about a person's TV habits, note the number of TVs and the position of the remote controls. If the remote is kept within easy reach from the typical seat, that may indicate a high frequency of TV watching.

What a Great Deal of Sound May Mean

Positive	*Challenging*
easygoing	unable to communicate
connected to many things	does not like to be judged
able to cope with stress	needs to be stimulated constantly

What Very Little Sound May Mean

Positive	*Challenging*
able to focus	feels isolated
self-confident	self-centered

SCENT

The nose is never asleep and never forgets. In fact, smells associated with childhood can conjure up entire scenes in the mind because the olfactory sensor is made up of brain cells and can store information. The pungent, warm aroma of cinnamon always makes me feel emotionally secure because it recalls the memory of my Grandma's apple pies. Someone else might be catapulted back to a specific point in time complete with remembered people, places, and activities by the simple scent of a rose. My Florida beach community's well water leaves a sulfur odor in the kitchen and bathrooms, that although pungent mentally transports me to my delightful oceanside home and therefore is a somewhat pleasant smell to me rather than foul, as it is to most people.

Aside from private memories of smell, scents move us emotionally, with certain odors triggering fairly consistent responses in all people. Therefore, choosing to live with a particular fragrance may communicate what a person needs or relates to. For example, lavender is often a favorite of older women. It is, among other things, an antiaphrodisiac and may be appropriate for many at this stage of life.

Categories of Scent and Their Meanings

Floral smells (roses, gardenias, violets, etc.) evoke desires for excitement and close relationships.

Ethereal scents (pear, banana) exude a feeling of groundedness and stability and may be selected by someone who does not like change.

Acrid scents (metals, vinegar) may personify one who is constrained, discerning, and likes to think and solve problems.

Minty scents (cedar, pine, peppermint) can indicate one who is creative and innovative but who can be impatient.

Musk (musk) is a scent not unlike a pheromone, and those who use it are broadcasting sexuality.

If you discover that a potential lover has a strong preference for one fragrance and either wears it or uses it in his or her home regularly, you can determine what he or she either likes or wants to overcome. Upon discovering that a lover uses a particular scent you can know that on some level he or she is expressing a need or desire. Here are a few examples.

What Using Specific Scents May Mean

Rose may mean one likes to nurture or needs strengthening of spirit.

Lavender may indicate a need to be detached, sedated, clear, or relaxed.

Mint may mean one needs a mental stimulant or feels shy.

Cedar may mean that one is trying to overcome feeling fearful.

Musk may mean a desire to be sexy.

Much has been written lately about pheromones, chemical substances that when smelled influence behavior. Although we aren't conscious of smelling another person's pheromone, it does influence how we feel about him or her. I had a friend whose engagement was broken off by her fiancé when he declared his dislike of her natural smell. A general rule of thumb is that if you don't like another's body scent, it is best to avoid pursuing a relationship no matter what other compelling attributes he or she may have.

TOUCH

 The chi of touch is extremely subtle because direct tactile contact with others is dictated by what our culture teaches us is appropriate. In many ways, we compensate for the lack of direct tactile sensation by storing mental associations between how things look and how they typically feel. The look of a plush velvet chair invites us to sit down, while one made from heavy, oily synthetic fibers does not. When viewing any scene, note whether or not you feel like you want to touch. Providing materials and fabrics that invite touching may project the desire to connect emotionally. Extreme examples are prisons, which avoid all soft textures, and houses of ill repute, which have nothing but deliciously sensuous fibers covering most furniture.

What Soft-to-the-Touch Upholstery May Mean

Positive	Challenging
sensuous	overly concerned with own feelings
empathetic	too emotional
self-contained	egotistical

What Rough-to-the-Touch Upholstery May Mean

Positive	Challenging
practical	emotionally distant
focused on things outside of self	unfriendly
other-directed	does not nurture self

In conclusion, chi is the vitality of all senses. It is through sensory experiences that we absorb the outside world. If the feel, sight, sound, or smell of a space is unappealing to you, it might indicate a person's unsuitability. If there is little to see, hear, feel, or smell, be sensitive to why sensorial experiences are being avoided. Often the chi of a space matches a person's emotional and physical energies.

Common sense will help you interpret how another's chi may help or hinder a relationship. If you come from a close-knit family, like a great deal of activity, and are likely to hug a friend who visits, a home without family photographs, sound, and movement can tip you off to a difference between the occupant and you. All my life I listened to public radio every morning. Brushing my teeth and eating breakfast seemed strange without the refrain of "All Things Considered." My morning coffee was incomplete without this chi. Unfortunately, I once had a roommate who hated any sound until after breakfast. An apparently minor difference underscored vastly different needs, and we lasted a very short time as roommates.

Chi is the force that vitalizes life. Do not dismiss any sensorial experience, because life is propelled by chi. In most cases a compromise on a fundamental chi issue will backfire in time. When in doubt, it is far better to err on the side of more chi and live with increased sensorial experiences. Life begets life.

7

THE BA-GUA: IT'S AS SIMPLE AS 1, 2, 3, 4, 5, 6, 7, 8, 9

A ba-gua is an octagonal shape that can be superimposed over any room or house to define areas most likely to evoke specific emotions. According to the Chinese, the physical world is a map for our emotional life and what is observed in each area can express much about a person's internal life. Although traditional feng shui uses the ba-gua as an overlay for an entire house, the pyramid school of feng shui tends to overlay the ba-gua map room by room. A space is divided into nine areas, eight sections at the perimeter and one in the center. An ancient tool, the ba-gua can be used to help determine what specific areas in life are actualized, damaged, or in need of focus or balance.

I am awestruck by the ability of the ancient Chinese to divine knowledge that we are only today confirming. Why the Chinese

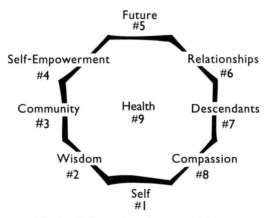

The implied meaning of space: the ba-gua.

selected an octagon to represent a room is a mystery since few then or now have eight-sided rooms. Only recently scientists determined that the smallest particle of matter is octagonal. Somehow the Chinese intuitively selected as an expression of all living spaces the shape that represents the most minute portion of matter.

> **The placement of objects and furniture in a room sheds light on how a person functions.**

The placement of objects and furniture in a room can highlight areas of strength or weakness. For example, if a potential partner does not have a place to sit in the ba-gua's relationship area in a main room, you may rightly conclude that he or she might not be ready to accept the responsibilities of an alliance. If there is not a sturdy table or chair placed inside and to the right of an entrance door, you may uncover a person not focused on supporting or nurturing others. Learning what the different segments in a room relate to can help uncover information not easily accessible.

HOW TO USE THE SEGMENTS OF THE BA-GUA TO UNDERSTAND A PERSON'S TRUE NATURE

Determining which furniture and objects have been positioned in different sections of the ba-gua can help you identify a person's strengths or weaknesses. By being able to align the message of empty spaces, clutter, or unusual symbols to an emotional or social sphere, you can discern another's assets or liabilities. In your own home you can shuffle or reprioritize areas of life that are troublesome by shifting furniture and accessories from one area to another. If, for example, a lover is selfish, activating the compassion area of the ba-gua in your bedroom will focus attention on emotions that harvest thoughtfulness.

> **Locating activities in the appropriate ba-gua areas can help reverse deficiencies and augment strengths.**

To get the desired results, you can use the actual area that relates to the ba-gua or the one across from it. For example, placing icons of partnership in the relationship area can speed your intention to find a mate. However, if working on the actual area does nothing to shift the energy, try focusing on the opposite area. Therefore, to find a relationship, cultivate your own wisdom. To enhance self-empowerment, focus on being compassionate to others. To be certain that you will be remembered for your good deeds, seek to strengthen your community. To stop worrying about the future, focus on yourself in the here and now.

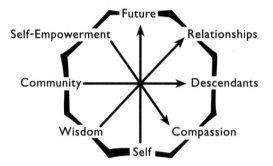

Activating an area of the ba-gua can impact on the opposite area.

It is best to apply the ba-gua on a room-by-room basis. To accurately lay the ba-gua over a room, place the position of self at the most frequently used entrance to that particular room. Therefore, standing at the entrance of any room places you in the self position. If the entrance door is off center, the surrounding areas (wisdom and compassion) are unequal.

Note if a particular location is messy, empty, cluttered, or otherwise different in appearance from the rest of the room. For example, if there is no furniture, wall hanging, or art object in the compassion area of a room, be alert to the possibility that this person is self-involved and would not likely be attentive to your needs. If you notice that there are stacks of papers or clutter in the self-empowerment area of a room, you may be picking up the fact that this person still has difficulty functioning at his or her peak.

Notice if there are any unusual symbols. When my sister's personal relationship was disintegrating, she moved an *Annie Get Your Gun* sculpture to the relationship corner of her living room. The papier-mâché Annie was aiming a rifle at a target, just as my sister was mentally ready to blast her present partner from her life. When

I pointed this out to her, she realized that she did in fact want to disengage herself from her present relationship. In this case the symbol revealed a desire.

Consider if choices are appropriate. I once went on a charity house tour and was rendered speechless by what I saw in one home. Greeting visitors at the entrance, facing all seating areas, and even in the kitchen hung nude oil paintings of the woman of the house. Granted, no one could help feeling envious because she was in peak physical condition, but it was not hard to guess how self-centered she may have been, needing to exhibit herself throughout her home. What strikes you as odd usually is.

Signs of Trouble in Any Area of the Ba-gua

too many objects or furnishings (clutter)

emptiness or lack of appropriate items (one chair at a dining table)

messy (papers spilling onto the floor near a desk, unfinished projects scattered all over)

an object out of place (games in the self-empowerment area, a desk in the relationship area)

an unusual symbol (a sword in the compassion area or a photograph of a former lover by the bed)

OVERVIEW OF ALL BA-GUA AREAS

The ba-gua or implied meaning of space

Self (#1)

The entrance to a space is critical, for this first impression is often lasting and powerful. I remember being with my mother when we found the house that was to become my childhood home. A fire was roaring in the fireplace, and the smell of burning pine needles created an aroma that I found intriguing because of my city upbringing. Even though it has been decades since I have lived there, the memory of that first impression remains. The point of entrance is experienced deeply and can shape lasting impressions.

Signs to Look for in the Self Area

Positive	*Challenging*
area rug	slippery flooring
adequate lighting	no nearby light switch or lamp
bell or sound device on a door	lock that sticks
something intriguing ahead	nothing to look at
welcoming picture such as a relaxing nature scene	artwork that frightens or intimidates

Wisdom or Self-Cultivation (#2)

Wisdom is the ability to extrapolate the essence from all things. A wise person gets the message instead of just the facts. Don't confuse wisdom with knowledge, for the two are distinctly different. Just as one can read a foreign language but not understand it, wisdom is more than spouting facts.

> **Wisdom comes from being willing to learn from every experience.**

Becoming wise requires self-cultivation. Many of life's rewards are reaped by improving ourselves. Interestingly, this area, to the left of an entrance door, is often the most underused spot in a room. Consider what you have placed on the floor and the walls to the left of any entrance door because what we place there often represents the ways in which we develop our potential.

Duke, a would-be writer, positioned his childhood desk at the left of his home's main entrance. He pours manuscripts out like tap water but does not have the fortitude to postpone gratification to edit one to completion. Noting the childhood desk in his wisdom area might make you suspicious when for the umpteenth time he pulls out a poem, story, or essay for you to read that he is just on the brink of finishing. You might find that this type will promise you the world and deliver very little. Like his desk, his ability to actualize remains at a child's level.

Discovering how much attention is paid to this area and what symbols are placed there will allow you to see how important it is for an individual to cultivate the self.

Signs to Look for in the Wisdom Area

Positive	Challenging
books, manuals, to-do lists	nothing that engages attention
stereo equipment, musical instruments	TV
reading chair	clutter
plants, fish tank, birdcages	photographs of the past
	uncared-for plants

Community (#3)

Community implies connections and dependence. Just as an infant depends on a caretaker, we all rely on a mammoth support system for survival. We are not meant to be separated from others, and the more we are disconnected, the less we are able to partake of our rich, full potential, which thrives when supported. Losing connections to others imprisons us and subjects us to the most severe form of punishment, isolation.

How invested a person is in a network or support system is revealed in the community area of the ba-gua. An empty community area will often be found in the home of someone who does not have lifelong friendships and may be estranged from his or her extended family and for whom office parties, block associations, or clubs are of little interest.

Signs to Look for in the Community Area

Positive	Challenging
telephone	empty
computer or fax	divider screen
two or more chairs	solo chair
service awards	sports trophies
files for volunteer projects	diaries or journaling albums

Self-Empowerment (#4)

We feel empowered and content when involved in activities we love. When you don't support your talents, proclivities, and desires, life can seem empty. It is far better for both parties in a relationship to be engaged in satisfying activities; therefore it is better to know if you have selected a partner who is paying attention to empowering his or her life. Look carefully in a bedroom, home office, or any private space to determine if the self-empowerment area is cultivated.

> **The more you are tuned in to your passion, the more likely you will be able to design your happiness.**

The key to contentment lies in feeling self-empowered. Self-empowerment is knowing that we can satisfy our aspirations by having the ability to function at our peak. When we are in our power, we are likely to make better companions.

> **Feeling empowered gives us the boost we need to satisfy our aspirations.**

Often significant furniture, such as a desk, reading chair, or sofa, will be placed in the self-empowerment corner in the homes of actualized people. My sister, Robyn, has a den with no place for furniture in the self-empowerment corner. Yet she has hung a stunning, valuable oil painting of a family on that wall. Knowing my sister as I do, I am aware that a primary relationship is extremely important for her to thrive. My sister's self-empowerment is enmeshed with her having an intimate family life.

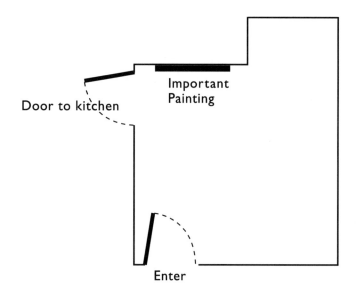

If there is no room for furnishings in an area, look for messages in the artwork.

Another friend has pictures of angels throughout her self-empowerment area. Placing these benevolent guardians in the self-empowerment section indicates her desire to be mentored or protected. She would not flourish with someone who was self-absorbed or had little energy to inspire her. Pay attention to the subject of artwork in the self-empowerment area, because it may illuminate what is needed to thrive. What is placed in the self-empowerment area often reveals how one tackles reaching personal goals.

> **The artwork placed on the self-empowerment wall often indicates what the owner needs to thrive.**

Signs to Look for in the Self-Empowerment Area

Positive	Challenging
comfortable chair	frayed or unkempt furnishings
hobby table or desk	unfinished long-term projects
diplomas or awards	piles of clutter or peeling paint
objects made by occupant	broken equipment
healthy plants or a fish tank	diseased or dying plants

Future (#5)

We rarely worry about the present moment, for we are usually busy dealing with it. The future, on the other hand, provokes anxiety for many. While the future is always just out of reach, it looms before us, as does the future position in the ba-gua.

Much of what we worry about encompasses what might happen. If I were to ask you to name three things with which you are currently concerned, the answer would likely be about what might happen. Unknowns make us feel insecure. What is chosen to adorn the walls and space of the future area often expresses what is wished for or feared. Salespersons who keep sales charts in their office's future area are expressing subconsciously that they are only as good as their current performance.

> **What is chosen to adorn the walls of the future area expresses what is wished for or feared.**

Most of the day I face a window positioned in the future area of my office. When a window coupled with lack of space precludes placing objects in an area, look outside and see if something has been added. I have an herb garden and a bird feeder positioned outside the window in the future area. The growth of plants mimics the growth I desire to achieve as I move forward in life, and the birds that fly to the feeder bring activity to the future area, which I hope to infuse with maximum vitality. Both symbols represent an optimistic view of what lies ahead.

Signs to Look for in the Future Area

Positive	Challenging
artwork depicting dreams and achievements	photos of the past
bed with the covers in place	bar stool
desk that is used for ongoing projects	file cabinet with inactive files
healthy plants	dying or diseased plants
objects that move	dust or mold
positive affirmation of goals via pictures, words, or images	boxes for storage of unused items

Relationships (#6)

The way we relate to others can contribute mightily to our overall happiness. It is imperative to determine a person's capacity to relate to others before opening one's heart. You should hesitate to invest your emotions in a person with no intimate friendships from the past and few in the present. Patterns of relating can sometimes be detected in a room's relationships area. Take, for example, Selma, a client who at the writing of this book had just ended a fourth marriage. Even though she was an avid collector of flat art, there were none hanging in her relationships area in her living room. "I just can't find any painting that is right for that area," she said when I urged her to hang something on that wall. Even after specifically purchasing a significant oil painting to hang on the relationships wall, when she brought it home she decided to put it elsewhere. Was Selma ready for another relationship? Probably not, and if she became involved, it most likely would not last.

Signs to Look for in the Relationships Area of a Room

Positive	Challenging
two chairs	empty
recent photos of family members	screen or divider
game table	work area
stash of gifts	cartons of old papers
art depicting two of anything	empty walls
flower arrangements or plants	paintings or a statue of a solitary person

Descendants (#7)

The single strongest biological urge of any species is to reproduce to leave a genetic imprint in the next generation. In humans it matters less if our influence is expressed by progeny, friends, colleagues, ideas, or deeds. What is normal is to desire to be remembered for some positive contribution and to be honored for inspiring future generations. Homes of those who spend time volunteering and doing good deeds or those who have a vested interest in helping their own children succeed will often have many items representing what might be their future contribution in a room's descendants area.

By observing what is placed in this general area, you can judge how committed a person is to the future, through family, friends, and good deeds. A person who invests time, energy, and talent to leave an imprint on the future is one who will be careful to interact today with grace, compassion, and concern.

> **How committed a person is to a long-term relationship can be noted in the descendants area.**

Helen and Rose are the parents of Theo, on whom they dote and pour their affections. Their home, while being a sophisticated New York pad, is filled with a multitude of toys, gadgets, costumes, and goodies for Theo and his friends. It is no surprise that this stash is placed in the descendants area of their main gathering room. Those without children will often have the descendants area filled with plants, photographs, light, favorite artwork, and books other than objects designed to entertain, like a game table or a TV.

Signs to Look for in the Descendants Area of a Room

Positive	Challenging
photographs or photo albums of children	dressing table
credenza or table	photograph of self
sofa	reclining chair
chess or checkerboard or a game table	exercise equipment
healthy plants	dartboard, crossword puzzles
lamp or spotlight	jigsaw puzzles

Compassion (#8)

Compassion provides us with the sensitivity to identify or empathize, thereby safeguarding the prospect of having successful relationships. When operating from deep caring, we motivate positive responses from others.

The compassion area is located to the right of the entrance to a room. In some cases a home or apartment may have two entrances, one used by the occupants and one the guests. Only consider the entrance a guest would normally use to determine your potential partner's compassion toward others. To evaluate the compassion directed at himself or herself, observe the entrance the owner uses daily. Be certain to note if equal attention is paid to both areas. If not, note where the emphasis is placed. If there are few or no positive signs in a guest's compassion entrance area, this may be someone who will disregard your needs.

> **A person who pays little attention to placing appropriate items in the compassion area will likely be inattentive to your concerns.**

Signs to Look for in the Compassion Area

Positive	Challenging
table for placing objects temporarily	clutter on a table
coat hooks or partially empty closet	no comfortable lighting
a place to sit down	breakable artifacts
umbrella stand	no place for personal belongings
chair	empty

Health—Physical, Mental, and Spiritual (#9)

In the same way as the most important organs in our body are positioned in the center, a room with an empty or defective center indicates a person's malfunctioning in physical, mental, or spiritual health. Vitality is missing when the center of a room has few significant accessories or furnishings or is totally empty. In some ways this area is the most important part of a room to observe, because it suggests the status of a person's well-being.

> **Physical, mental, or spiritual vitality is a concern when the center of a room is empty.**

In a bedroom where a double bed typically extends into the center, observe the details of a bed's cover, the choice of sheets, and the objects at the foot of the bed, such as a trunk, table, or bedspread holder. The more details you see, the more attention the occupant is paying to physical, emotional, or spiritual health. Those who do not make their bed up or have little bed decor often have the most physical, mental, or spiritual problems.

Signs to Look for in the Health Area of a Room

Positive	Challenging
vibrant, patterned carpets	unpatterned flooring with no furniture on it
artifacts and objects on a cocktail table	an empty cocktail table
any seating units	clutter
lighting focused on the center	insignificant or undersized light or furnishings

GROUPING CATEGORIES OF A BA-GUA

Sections of a ba-gua can be grouped together to give a general overview instead of pinpointing one area. Sometimes a door or window makes it impractical to place anything in an area. If the space is difficult because there are many doors or windows, using these broad categories can expose some problems or gifts a person may have.

Broad Categories of the Ba-gua

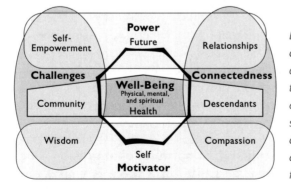

By grouping three contiguous areas of the ba-gua together, we arrive at five sections of a space that are controlled by distinctly different factors.

Power Area: Self-Empowerment, Future, and Relationships

In a confined space, the wall farthest from the entrance to a room is the power wall. Facing out from this position, you have the most time to react and the greatest distance away from anyone who enters. You are empowered because you are in the best position to protect yourself. While you may not need physical protection today, humans have depended upon time and space to flee danger. We are more powerful when farthest from an entrance to a space.

Along the far wall from left to right lie self-empowerment, future, and relationships. To reach your own level of mastery, to be free from worry, and to have intimate emotional support from your peers are the three forms of power we strive for. Therefore the decor near and on the power wall can reveal an occupant's feelings about life.

> **Those who feel satisfied with life will usually place at least one treasured item on the power wall.**

Signs to Look for in the Power Area

Positive	Challenging
diploma, awards, or trophies	empty
representations of one's area of expertise	piles of unread reading materials
large or exotic plants	past vacation photographs
rare or personally valued artifacts	old yearbooks
computers, workbenches, or desks put to use	photos or mementos of former accomplishments

Connectedness Area: Relationships, Descendants, and Compassion

Ninety percent of the human species is right-hand dominant. Scientists could not find a left-handed gene and finally discovered that left-handedness is caused by a mother's elevated levels of hormones triggered by stress during pregnancy. Most left-handed people feel almost as comfortable on the right side as right-handers. We shake, hug, and gravitate toward the right when physically connecting with another human being. In moments of panic, such as when we lose our balance, most of us extend our right hand ahead of the left to break a fall. Human beings connect with objects in the world and with others with greater ease on the right side of their bodies and prefer to gravitate toward the right side of a room. Objects on the left side of a room are used less than those on the right.

> **The capacity for deep attachments is revealed when there are items which provide comfort placed in a room's connection area.**

People who are connected to the lives of others (relationships), connected in a meaningful way to impacting the future (descendants), and connected empathetically to others (compassion), can be ideal partners. What is on the right side of a room can reveal the capacity for deeply rooted attachments.

Signs to Look for in the Connection Area

Positive	Challenging
seating for more than one	cabinets with doors closed
coat racks	storage units
paintings with more than one person	somber or depressing themes in paintings

brightest lighting or colors
   in a room

black marble, walls, or
   curtains

replicas of houses, street scenes

landscapes bereft of people

gaming tables

bookkeeping area

photographs of family
   and friends

photographs without
   people

The relationships, descendants, and compassion group relies on connections to sustain it. If you care about having intimate relationships, spend time working toward creating something beneficial for the future, and are concerned with how others feel, you are motivated by issues of connection.

Motivator or Entrance Area: Wisdom, Self, and Compassion

The entrance wall is a springboard for all experiences. The entry determines how a person proceeds and sets a tone that is hard to alter. The entrance to a space can be likened to birth, and its experience can set in motion a feeling about a person that is hard to alter.

The experience of entering a home consists of crossing three thresholds. Threshold number one is the first view of the home. There is a moment of recognition, an instant when you say "ah-hah" as you round a corner or get close enough to see part of the property or building that is home. Whether you approach your home from an unassuming back door or a beautifully manicured front lawn, the feeling evoked by arriving home will be influenced by whatever positive or negative associations you have with being there. How other people experience your home, however, will not be filtered through such associations. There are always different routes leading to an address. Which one do you give to your home? Is it the most convenient, the most scenic, or the most interesting? A pragmatist will give the shortest route, a dreamer the most enthralling, and a nurturer the most detailed directions.

The second threshold begins when tactile contact is made. Starting down a path, knocking on a door, or turning a key to open a lock is the first tactile connection made with a home. Is there a heavy door knocker, giving a sense of permanence? Does a key work efficiently, without grinding? Is a doormat thick and sturdy enough to remove debris from the bottom of shoes or thin and likely to bunch up when walked on? Since the entrance is not only used every day but also prepares us for the experience inside, the more ill kept it is, the more likely there is a lack of concern for others.

The last encounter is one experienced after stepping inside. It is visceral, with the scent of place filling the nostrils and a thermal reaction to the appropriateness of the temperature. What you are responding to is the intimate realm of place, and if you don't feel right, be wary. Sometimes this first experience alone is enough to warn you to be cautious.

Where we are encouraged to proceed next is telling. Are you guided toward a kitchen, a gathering room, or a special room? Are you offered a snack or asked to sit down? The first experience of place communicates a great deal about what the resident believes motivates others. How you are ushered into a home can be the harbinger for future personal interaction.

The entrance wall sets a tone for and supports subsequent actions. In this sense it motivates and is a springboard for how one lives. Wisdom or self-cultivation and compassion provoke most of life's actions and therefore are important aspects of interpersonal relationships. It is far more satisfying to be involved with someone who is compassionate, who can be empathetic and care about how he or she interfaces with others.

Signs to Look for in the Motivator Area

Positive	Challenging
pleasant scents	stacks of unopened mail
table to place things on	answering machine
fresh flowers	no area rug or distinctive flooring
books and magazines	any delicate or easy-to-break object
doorbell with pleasant sound or substantial knocker	garbage pail
sconces or wall lights	no light switch
fish tank, birdhouse	animal feeding station or cat litter box

**The wisdom, self, and compassion
group motivates a solid relationship.**

If you are the first one to visit a sick friend, tend to be focused on the present, and love to continue to learn and develop, you are self-motivated and a catalyst for your own and others' growth.

**Challenges Area: Wisdom/Self-Cultivation, Community,
and Self-Empowerment**

The three contiguous areas on the left side of the ba-gua are the most challenging to perfect, as is using the left hand for most of us. That which is difficult is often avoided. However, wisdom/self-cultivation, community, and self-empowerment create strong supports for life and provide a framework supporting a meaningful life, so this part of every room deserves attention.

When we are challenged to notice and extend beyond our comfort zone, we journey on a road often dreamed of and rarely traveled. Those who focus on the left side of a space have remarkable abilities to meet challenges and change them into opportunities.

Signs to Look for in the Challenges Area

Positive	*Challenging*
visually indicated future goals	past achievements
biographies	many different tasks in progress (sewing and unfinished letters)
salmon or green colors	regal, deep colors, especially purple or royal blue

Well-Being Area: Physical, Mental, and Spiritual Health

We cannot disregard our physical, mental, and spiritual health if we wish to thrive. The center of a room represents our vitality in critical arenas of life.

Signs to Look for in the Well-Being Area

Positive	Challenging
valued rugs, artwork	broken artifacts
pristinely clean	stained or worn-out carpeting
healthy plants	
current newspapers	out-of-date periodicals

OTHER BA-GUA CONSIDERATIONS

Unusual Objects

Notice the placement of all unusual objects. For example, a client had a sculpture of a warrior with shield and spear held menacingly in front. It was different from all other artwork in her home and was positioned in the self-empowerment corner of her gathering room. It said she was apt to go to any lengths to achieve her goals, including using those she perceived thwarted her chances of ascending the corporate ladder. Where unusual items are placed can reveal a great deal.

Collections

Collections can disclose much about a person. Note what they are and if they are placed in one room or several. For example, my uncle Mike was a stamp collector and kept the major part of his collection under lock and key in the community area in his spare bedroom. He also had one treasured album with stamps that he had traveled to the locations to buy. He kept that in his bedroom dresser, which was also in the community area. Choosing these spots couldn't express him more succinctly. Not wanting to be sociable, he preferred that my aunt go to parties and out to dinner without him while he spent his time with his collection. His stamp collection was his community and what he related to best.

In conclusion, the implied meaning of space or ba-gua is a useful tool in highlighting both positive and challenging qualities in a person. Observing the choices made for different areas can help you get to the root of a person's issues. For example, if an area rug with a triangular pattern is chosen for the center of a room, be on the lookout for some volatile health issues. If low, heavy square shapes are chosen for the descendants area, that person may be relying too heavily on children or friends.

It is not by accident that we place furniture, objects, and lighting where we do. It feels most comfortable in the positions we choose because it expresses what is inside. The ba-gua is a powerful tool when used to peer inside another's soul.

8

THE ELEMENTS

The elements fire, earth, metal, water, and wood are used in feng shui to describe all objects in a physical environment. Look around. Everything you see is made up of three of these elements (earth, metal, and wood) and has been formed by one of the other two (fire and water). Only plastics and fabrics might not be easily recognizable as an element, but even plastics are considered the earth or metal element and fabrics either a wood element (when made from plants) or a metal element (when made from synthetic materials).

Every object needs a catalyst (fire and water) to form it—either actual fire or the heat from a physical action or liquid (water). For example, a carved wood chair requires the heat of a machine or human action to carve it, while paper needs water added to wood. Although both are wood elements, the former would be considered wood/fire, the latter wood/water. The catalyst determines how an element will be experienced by others.

People are not objects, but all animate and inanimate entities inhabit the same world, so a relationship with the earth's elements can be seen in people too. Human beings evolved from the same natural laws governing all things. It is therefore reasonable to think that we are expressed in similar ways. I leave it to geneticists and psychologists to unravel the mystery of why some of us are born brave or musically talented. It is simply my contention that we, in a general sense, are not distinctly different from all that exists on the physical plane. By examining the broadest characteristics ascribed to each element, we come up with a group's characteristics, which predict how a person who is similar to an element will interface with his or her surroundings.

Personalities, like physical objects, are usually motivated by an element and a catalyst. Those with only an element and no catalyst may find themselves unable to actualize themselves as easily as those who have both an element and a catalyst. With a catalyst it is possible to understand a person's preferences and the way he or she is likely to feel comfortable. For example, a wood/fire person would be expansive, as is wood, and reactive, as is fire. If a wood/fire person were your lover and you wanted to introduce him to your family, it might be better to do so in a restaurant, rather than at home. A wood personality with a fire emotion might feel less threatened with more space around him. On the other hand, a wood/water type may feel better in an intimate setting, for water types are likely to want more intimacy and contact. A wood/water lover would best meet your family at a dinner party in a home.

How we act and how we feel are often different. Our personality is the outer layer and our emotions the inner. Later in this chapter there is a test to help you uncover which elements express your personality and which express your emotions. These will be called your *expressed element* (personality) and *hidden element* (emotions). More than likely one element will be slightly dominant in each category. It is possible and even probable that your expressed element will be different from your hidden element or that your personality and your emotions each will reflect more than one element. The more elements you have, the easier it will be to forge life's path. On the road to actualization, we should accumulate all elemental characteristics. Those who do are often the most content.

The way one acts and feels is similar to the expression of one or more of the five elements.

Each element is associated with a shape, color, texture, direction, smell/taste, sound, season, and aspects of human behavior. For example, it is reasonable to associate fire with vivaciousness, hot temper, and energy considering how flames leap, whether from a candle or a raging inferno. Here's what is associated with fire and why:

Triangle—the shape of a flame, considered the least stable shape

Red—the color with the longest wavelength, which attracts the most attention

Rough textures—when it doesn't consume completely, fire leaves surfaces jagged and rough

South—in the northern hemisphere, south is the direction of warm weather; fire is associated with warmth

Spicy—hot spices burn the inside of the mouth or make us sweat as does fire

Cymbals—an unexpected crash can make one leap with surprise as can touching a flame

When we know a person's elemental configuration, we can predict how he or she will respond in a given situation. Fire types will not tolerate frustration without a lot of fuss, while water types are apt to let stress roll off their backs like waves lapping onto the shore. Fire's high energy generates sharp sensations and is similar to intense reactions, like moving quickly. Fire types often find themselves embroiled in all kinds of drama because their reactions are not always thought out.

When you know which elemental type a person is, you will be able to figure out what elements to place in an environment to make him or her comfortable. Before we can examine our elemental selves, let's look at each element's attributes. The following list associates each element with its shape, color, texture, direction, smell/taste, sound, and season. These are the tools to use when adjusting an environment. For example, to get a fiery type to change an opinion, add the water element, which includes choices such as a bouquet of black tulips, an open-weave blue afghan tossed over a sofa, or ethereal harp or violin music.

ELEMENT	SHAPE	COLOR	TEXTURE	DIRECTION	SMELL	SOUND	SEASON
FIRE	▲	Red	Rough	South	Bitter	Cymbals	Summer
EARTH	■	Terra-cotta	Firm	Center	Floral Musk Sweet	Drums	May September
METAL	●	Reflective White, Gold, Silver, Copper	Smooth Slippery	West	Acrid	Xylophone Piano	Fall
WATER	〰	Black, Blue	Open Weave	North	Ethereal	Harp Violin	Winter
WOOD	▮	Green	Grainy	East	Minty Resinous	Reeds Horns	Spring

When the senses are stimulated by an element's qualities, we react in the same way as we would if experiencing the element. For example, water nourishes wood; therefore, having water symbols, colors, shapes, and sounds in an environment will make a wood type feel nourished and give him or her the energy needed to pursue goals. If you desire to be with a person who expresses earth's characteristics, add fire, because fire excites earth.

Since psychology, astrology, and other fields have categorized human behavior broadly, it is not unreasonable to group human tendencies by using the five elements. In fact, the five elements have been used successfully to identify and treat illnesses in Chinese medicine for thousands of years. By understanding typical responses to place, we can broaden our personal resources and increase the possibility for each of us to align ourselves with someone who is likely to be in accord with our elemental nature. The following chart gives a general overview of characteristics associated with each element.

General Positive Characteristics Associated with Elements

Fire—charged, competitive, energetic, enthusiastic, vivacious, charismatic, and passionate

Earth—steadfast, loyal, consistent, realistic; likes to explore in depth, values family and community, and serves as peacemaker

Metal—intense, thorough, easily fascinated, focused, discerning, serious, and refined

Water—sympathetic, reflective, yielding, accommodating, honest, insightful, empathetic, self-sufficient, and persistent

Wood—flexible, inquisitive, rarely bored, thorough, accepting; does well under pressure

General Challenging Characteristics Associated with Elements

 Fire—excitable, combative, reactive, quick-tempered, easily bored, tending to overindulge

 Earth—stubborn, risk averse, rejecting of new ideas, uncomfortable with change, greedy, manipulative

 Metal—defensive, withdrawn, arrogant, picky, emotionally uninvolved

 Water—overemotional, easily hurt, emotionally needy, temperamental, self-indulgent, rash, critical, and secretive

 Wood—demanding, fault finding, arrogant, judgmental, opportunistic, and impatient

More often than not, a person who is uncomfortable with one element's qualities will not have its components (from the chart on page 93) at home. Conversely, too much of one element in a home may point to a person who has too few other elemental characteristics. Look for extremes to uncover an elemental imbalance.

How One Element Affects Another

Have you ever tried to light a match on a windy day? In general, elements have a positive or challenging relationship to each other. It's not that you absolutely cannot light a match on a gusty day; it's just harder to accomplish it. By considering how one element actually affects another, you can deduce how a particular environment will affect a person. One of my students, who expressed dissatisfaction with her marriage, had created a bedroom with an overwhelming amount of fire. With red walls, shiny surfaces, and hard angles, she was unconsciously using fire's agitation to make her wood-type husband extremely uncomfortable. She was literally burning him up. By tweaking elemental balances you can manipulate a relationship.

How elements in an environment affect us depends on what element we are. My friend Alison is a water person. She is easygoing and slow to form opinions, she can understand both sides of a conflict, and she is a natural mediator. Most times her water element serves her well, because her job is to maintain quality in a huge learning center, and her ability to mediate is a good resource. In her own life, however, her water aspect often keeps her from making clear-cut immediate decisions. Alison's private life would be helped considerably if she incorporated the fire element into her home. Fire would act as a stimulus to shake her out of inaction during times when action would be the better choice. Fire could spark her to make decisions. In her work space, however, speeding up her processes with fire might charge an otherwise mellow atmosphere. When appropriate, using an element that we do not possess abundantly can initiate change, growth, or movement.

WHY DISCOVER YOUR ELEMENTAL SELF?

Knowing the elements that compose your personality and emotions can be helpful when designing a space in which to thrive with another (and also alone, but that is not the subject of this book). Discerning the elements that someone has selected for an environment can unearth the person's true nature and help you gauge compatibility. During times when you need to adjust a relationship, you can add or discard the element that will control or exacerbate, support or suppress. Knowing what to place in a home to help expand the positive and diminish the negative can be vital in securing a long-term, life-affirming partnership.

Consider Norm, an articulate, engaging, and successful thirty-one-year-old salesman. Norm would strike you as an outgoing, sociable young man. Yet these qualities, normally associated with wood or metal, belie who he really is.

At thirty-one Norm has a winning personality, good looks, and financial success—so why isn't he married? The main gathering space in his home, although spacious and airy with little furniture, feels strangled and heavy. In front of a large tan leather sofa is a huge, chunky butcher-block coffee table. Its fat legs are planted firmly on a square area rug, and its top surface is piled high with popular men's magazines.

Although the general feeling is empty, the atmosphere is oddly torpid since Norm's home is filled with an overabundance of earth elements—the beige/brown colors, low, chunky furniture, and square rug. Blank walls exaggerate the room's grounded feeling because nothing diverts the eye up and away from the floor level. So much earth in Norm's environment suggests that although he doubtless possesses positive earth attributes of stability, steadfastness, and competence in a crisis, he is challenged by earth's attributes of stubbornness, resistance to change, and risk aversion.

All elements and people can coexist in either a physical or an emotional plane if surrounded, buffered, or infused with another element. If, for example, Norm met Alison, they might be frustrated with each other's inability to change. However, both could benefit by introducing the other's element into their environment, as well as the fire element. Adding that to a mutual environment would support a better relationship. If you are considering aligning yourself with someone who might not be the best element choice for you, I will suggest ways to alter a space to mitigate challenges and increase your potential as a team.

This book does not suggest that you avoid joining with someone whose elemental nature is challenging for you. What you will discover is how to adjust an environment to make it supportive no matter what your elemental combination might be. Small adjustments in an environment can benefit both you and a partner. Knowing how elements interact with each other can help prepare you for certain reactions and attitudes. If you are presently in a relationship, behaviors that may seem puzzling can be viewed in a new light. We are easier on others when we know that they are constitutionally inclined to express themselves in a certain way. With specific knowledge certain behaviors become less disturbing.

A home is a mirror of the self in so many ways, and to ignore the signs present in a home can prove disastrous. Gathering information about your own and another's elemental type will help you build a harmonious relationship.

THE ELEMENTS AND HOW TO CATEGORIZE THEM

Most of us gravitate toward a certain look or style. Open your closet and see if one color jumps out. Until I moved to Florida permanently, my closet's interior could have been photographed for a space odyssey entitled *Traveling Toward the Black Hole*. It was almost impossible to distinguish one black outfit from the next. Moreover, it seems uncanny, but every piece of artwork that I fall in love with and bring home seems to have a great deal of black. People tend to be consistent in their choices. Almost without exception, we make certain selections that unfold into a coherent theme.

You will be able to identify an elemental category by observing the overall look. A home with sleek, straight-lined contemporary furnishings is a wood environment, while a room furnished with art nouveau decor is water. Confirm this impression by seeing if the colors used match the ascribed element. If the sleek contemporary home's chairs are covered in forest green (green is wood's color), and the paintings contain images of forests or a big-city skyline (rectangles are wood's line), you have clear confirmation of the wood element. If the art nouveau decor (water) is in a room painted in glossy red (fire) and the paintings are of snow-capped Alpine mountains or birds in flight (fire), you have uncovered two elements for this person, water and fire.

WHAT IS YOUR ELEMENTAL NATURE?

Each of us has a public and a private persona. The obsequious employee can be a tyrant with his family; the hellion at school can be the obedient child at home. And even when there is less discernible distinction, know that there can be a rift between how we act and how we feel. Comedians are classic examples.

In his autobiography, Sid Caesar documented his long struggle with depression. The distance between his public persona and private one is as colossal as the Grand Canyon. What you see is not always what you get. Scope-ing makes discrepancies easier to grasp.

Three tests have been designed for this chapter, one to help you expose the element that represents your expressed self or personality, one to uncover your emotional elemental self, and one to help you determine if your elements are on the challenging side or not. While most healthy people express all elements at some time, we tend to have a propensity for one or two. These tests will help you determine which elements express you most forcefully, both outwardly and inwardly. People often alter segments of their personality to accommodate work situations, so take the tests from a personal, not professional, point of view.

When you take these tests, you will be answering the questions in the "threshold of consciousness," as Joseph Campbell called it— you will be describing yourself with full awareness of how you choose to respond. But that is not how we make our choices for our homes. Certainly we make conscious decisions to purchase this couch over that one, but it's the subconscious that dictates whether we repeatedly lean toward one element or another. The conscious contribution to our home choices may come from what Campbell termed the *persona*, Latin for "mask." Your persona may dictate the choice of one style of couch and your inner self another. To complicate matters, our personas are not fixed entities, but are subject to our acquired experiences coupled with our physiology and behavioral tendencies. We adjust ourselves either wholesale or in tiny increments to deal with the here and now. Today's test scores could shift as life experiences lead us. Also, most of us have more than one persona, such as an executive persona, a parent persona, a lover persona, and so on. Understanding which parts of you are guiding which choices will make you increasingly astute at interpreting the complicated choices that others make. (Keep in mind that for those who are unempowered to choose, as might be the case with people living with roommates, a person's home would not necessarily represent them.)

It is significant to note that in Winifred Gallagher's book *Just the Way You Are* she presents personality models as advanced by Paul Costa and Robert McCrae. Five basic personality types are described as extroversion, agreeableness, conscientiousness, neuroticism, and openness to experience. Can these five types not be likened to the five elements? Fire types can be associated with extroversion, while earth types are agreeable insofar as they often are looked upon as dependable. Metal types find their conscientiousness keeps them involved with a process. The neuroticism of water types is in the sense that they are always in flux, for water types can go with the flow. Finally, a wood type's expansiveness can easily be described as openness to experience.

Which type are you? Take this test, and perhaps give this test to a potential lover.

ELEMENT TEST 1: YOUR PERSONALITY OR EXPRESSED SELF

Answer either *yes* or *no*. Pick the answer that applies most often.

1. Do you plan what you'll get done each day and most often accomplish it?

2. Are you slow to form opinions and then reluctant to alter them?

3. Do you cry at most weddings, emotional movies, and happy events?

4. Are you constantly thinking, musing, or planning?

5. Do you tend to change brands of toothpaste, toilet paper, or laundry soap frequently?

6. Do you make up your mind quickly?

7. Do others seek your advice?

8. Is it easy for you to understand why some people display extreme emotions?

9. Are you able to hold your emotions in check most of the time and not reveal how you feel?

10. Is it hard for you to understand why some people cannot change a difficult situation?

11. Do you enjoy the process more than the results?

12. Are you unable to hold back expressing your opinion?

13. Do you thrive on competition and feel ambitious?

14. Are you content to spend time alone and not need to socialize all the time?

15. Are you the one in your family or circle of friends who likes to keep the peace?

ELEMENT TEST 2: YOUR EMOTIONAL OR HIDDEN SELF

Circle the letter of the answer that best describes you.

1. How do you feel about trying new ventures?

    a. I hate change.
    b. I welcome change.
    c. I rarely think about it.
    d. I love to plan for change.
    e. I like change, but it makes me a little anxious.

2. Do you reflect on decisions deeply before starting a new project?

    a. No, I tend to let the answer come to me intuitively.
    b. Yes, but I tend to strategize rather then reflect on whether I should or shouldn't.
    c. No, I jump right in and start doing.
    d. Yes, I tend to go over the positive and negative sides carefully before I decide.
    e. Yes, I consider how it will impact on my future and go ahead only if positive.

3. Which are your favorite activities?

    a. I like to build from scratch (carpentry, baking, sewing, etc.).
    b. I like to invent or play mental games (make up tests, do crossword puzzles, etc.).
    c. I like to play games of chance (commodities, stock market, or card games, etc.).
    d. I would like to be creative and build a concept (choreograph, write music, or direct plays, etc.).
    e. I like to be creative and literally hands on (cooking, working with clay, or gardening).

4. What do you worry about most?

    a. I imagine I get every disease that I read about.
    b. I worry I will be in a plane crash every time I travel.
    c. I get nervous that I will not be able to explain myself in tense or confrontational situations.
    d. I feel guarded and protective of my private thoughts.
    e. I worry about not getting things done.

5. How do you respond to illness?

   a. I tend to stay at home and recuperate.
   b. I seek advice from a trusted medical practitioner and methodically follow it.
   c. I tend to get depressed at the onset.
   d. I have the willpower to do whatever is needed to restore my health.
   e. I look at it as a challenge to beat.

6. What would you most like to do on a Saturday night?

   a. Enjoy solitude and spend time at home
   b. Enjoy going out with friends and talking about what's happened during the week
   c. Enjoy getting dressed up and going to a party
   d. Enjoy visiting with close friends or family
   e. Enjoy being with one friend or my spouse

7. I like others to know me as:

   a. patient and deep.
   b. powerful and confident.
   c. diplomatic and tactful.
   d. organized, tasteful, and discriminating.
   e. intuitive, funny, and optimistic.

8. When involved in something I like to do, I generally:

   a. like goals and guidelines stated explicitly.
   b. like to be sure that all involved are working in harmony.
   c. find that pressure doesn't distract me from doing the job well.
   d. will be patient and consistent until a job is completed.
   e. expect myself to be able to see new ways to do things.

9. I know deep down that I am:

   a. funny, empathetic, and fun.
   b. relaxed, loyal, and supportive.
   c. efficient, virtuous, and smart.
   d. self-sufficient, honest, and persevering.
   e. a leader, talented, and assertive.

ELEMENT TEST 3: POSITIVE OR CHALLENGING?

Answer *yes* or *no*.

1. Is a day incomplete unless you can exercise?

2. Do you feel a little bit angry about something at least once or twice a day?

3. Would you rather stay home than go out most nights?

4. Are you often the person a friend or family member calls on when in distress?

5. When you listen to people talk, are you frequently thinking about your response?

6. When you have a dilemma to resolve, can you think of many solutions quickly?

7. Do you dislike playing games that require mental speed?

8. If you are with a group of people and a prejudicial remark is made, can you detect through facial nuances and body language if one person in that group might be hurt?

9. Have you involved yourself with many different jobs, projects, and groups during the last 10 percent of your life?

10. Are you fearful of learning new things if they seem difficult?

Scoring Element Test 1

The first fifteen questions are designed to expose the elements through which your personality is expressed. It is the persona you're comfortable revealing to the world. Most likely you've been associated with the characteristics of this element from childhood. Add up the *yes* answers. The element that scores the highest is the one that is most obvious in your personality. If you have scored equally for two or more elements, your personality is more complex and includes the characteristics of those elements.

1. Yes = 1 for fire
2. Yes = 1 for earth
3. Yes = 1 for water
4. Yes = 1 for metal
5. Yes = 1 for wood

6. Yes = 1 for fire
7. Yes = 1 for earth
8. Yes = 1 for water
9. Yes = 1 for metal
10. Yes = 1 for wood
11. Yes = 1 for metal
12. Yes = 1 for fire
13. Yes = 1 for wood
14. Yes = 1 for water
15. Yes = 1 for earth

Count all *yes* answers and score the elements accordingly. For example, if you answered *yes* to numbers 1, 6, and 12, you are a +3 fire. If you answered *yes* to only number 1, you are a +1 fire. If you answered *no* to 1, 6, and 12, you are a 0 fire.

The more elements in your score, the more balanced you are. Cindy, a therapist, college professor, and yoga teacher who assisted me at my workshops at Kripalu Center in Lenox, Massachusetts, dashed up to me after I had given the class this test to ask me what scoring +3 for three (fire, metal, and water) elements meant. Having strong personality traits in three areas served Cindy well. Each area of her life required a different expression. As a therapist a water element would help her to empathy, patience, and nonjudgment. As a college professor the metal element would help her spark her student's mental activity and she would be able to think on her feet. Last, her fire element would be a perfect complement for teaching yoga. We are inspired to stretch our bodies not by someone who appears self-absorbed and lethargic, but by someone with the enthusiasm, fire's energy, and desire to inspire others.

Scoring Element Test 2

The following answers will reveal your emotional elements. These elements are hidden from casual contacts and are apparent only when someone gets to know you intimately. Deep within each of us are feelings and proclivities that we typically do not express publicly. Football star Rosie Grier stunned his public twenty years ago when he permitted himself to be photographed at one of his favorite hobbies, needlepoint. These answers will uncover emotional elements, those feelings we do not expose casually.

1. a. earth
   b. wood

      c. water

      d. metal

      e. fire

2.   a. water

      b. metal

      c. fire

      d. earth

      e. wood

3.   a. wood

      b. metal

      c. fire

      d. water

      e. earth

4.   a. fire

      b. metal

      c. wood

      d. earth

      e. water

5.   a. earth

      b. wood

      c. water

      d. metal

      e. fire

6.   a. water

      b. wood

      c. fire

      d. earth

      e. metal

7.   a. water

      b. wood

      c. earth

      d. metal

      e. fire

8.   a. metal

      b. earth

      c. wood

      d. water

      e. fire

9. a. fire
    b. earth
    c. metal
    d. water
    e. wood

The elements chosen the most are the ones that represent you. If you scored equally high for two elements on Test 1 and two elements on Test 2, you would have four potential elemental combinations. If, for example, you scored +2 fire and +2 earth on Test 2, your hidden elements are both fire and earth. If you also scored +2 fire and +2 metal in Test 1, you would be the following combinations: fire/earth, fire/fire, metal/earth, and metal/fire. *Read all the sections that apply to your combinations.*

More elements are better than fewer. A fully actualized person has all elements. When missing an element, know that it can be incorporated by adding its representation in your home. Even when you cannot give another of these tests, you can detect the elements by looking at the choices he or she has made. For example, my mother is the model of decorum. However, she has always incorporated the color red into her homes. Although her personality is refined, she expresses her emotional fire by selecting the color associated with it. The subconscious element can often be inferred from the environment if what is seen doesn't match the personality. When there is a color, line, sound, or smell that seems incongruous with one's outward nature, it probably represents the subconscious one.

Every element has the capacity to be either positive or challenging. Test 3 reveals if you have more assets or liabilities in both the personality and emotional elements revealed in the previous tests. Let's say you are a metal/fire person and Test 3 revealed you are positive in metal and challenged in fire; you would work on your emotional life more than how you come across to others.

Scoring Test 3

In the general description of the elements there are both positive and challenging characteristics. Test 3 will determine whether you lean to positive or challenging in your main elemental configuration. Many times you will answer two *nos* for an element, which means that you have the capacity to be either positive or challenged. This is normal; most of us can sometimes express the highest and best of the element and sometimes find ourselves with the more challenging aspects. However, this information is especially interesting if you find that a main element is challenged and not positive. In this case, you will want to work with the corresponding elements that affect or loosen the negative effect of the challenged element. For example, a challenged fire on an emotional level should have lots of earth or water in an environment. Fire types are reactive and can take offense easily or overreact. A lover who likes to tease could drive a challenged fire crazy. However, hanging a picture with a great deal of blue or a water theme could help a challenged fire type accept friendly teasing more easily. Use the information in Test 3 as an adjunct to both Tests 1 and 2.

1. Yes = positive fire
2. Yes = challenged fire
3. Yes = challenged earth
4. Yes = positive earth
5. Yes = challenged metal
6. Yes = positive metal
7. Yes = challenged water
8. Yes = positive water
9. Yes = challenged wood
10. Yes = positive wood

Finally, there are elemental types that are naturally more compatible. Just as wood can usually not withstand the onslaught of intense fire, wood personalities can be overwhelmed by fire types. However, a waterlogged tree or a wood/water type can deflect the sparks of fire with no trouble at all. Knowing the combination is important in determining which type is likely to be the most compatible for you. Remember, even when you are not elementally compatible, there are ways to position the elements in an environment to help you coexist happily.

All elements have the capacity for deeply satisfying, respectful relationships. It is just a matter of what you are willing to tolerate and how hard you are willing to work toward making a relationship work. Nature has no favorite elements. No type of element or elemental combination is best. Remember, if you are motivated, you will be successful at putting any combination together, and sometimes the most arduous road traveled will be infinitely more satisfying than one that is easier to forge.

9

FIRE TYPE

Shape: triangle—a flame's shape is a triangle

Color: reddish orange—fire's general appearance is red or deep orange

Texture: rough—when fire doesn't consume completely, it leaves surfaces jagged

Direction: south—in the northern hemisphere, south is the direction of warmer weather

Smell/Taste: bitter—spicy smells, the kind that cause you to react immediately

Sound: cymbals—an unexpected crash can make one leap with surprise as can touching a flame

Season: summer—the hottest months

Positive Characteristics of Fire

charged
competitive
energetic
enthusiastic
vivacious
quick to react and move
charismatic
passionate

Challenging Characteristics of Fire
excitable
combative
reactive
quick-tempered
easily bored
tending to overindulge

Partner Who Controls Fire
water, metal

Partner Who Balances Fire
earth

Partner Who Supports Fire
wood

Partner Who Is Supported by Fire
earth

Partner Who Is Restrained by Fire
water

OVERVIEW

A fire person has tremendous physical and intellectual energy and draws others to him or her just as a flame attracts the eye. Although quick to come to a conclusion, fire types can change their minds on a dime. Engulfed with energy until depleted, fire types give no warning before collapsing. Fire traits will be exaggerated and could make any situation incendiary when a fire type is surrounded by a red Oriental carpet, burgundy upholstered furniture, conical lamp shades, and art with triangular images.

Fire people tend to run, not walk, toward their latest goal. New trends either fascinate them or leave them cold. Typically there is no middle ground for those with a great deal of fire. If you want an enthusiastic partner and one who will be upbeat and willing to leap into new situations, a fire type is ideal.

Fire types also don't reflect on a situation before responding. They live in a spontaneous, open way and cannot tolerate restraints. Putting a fire type in a restrictive environment will either cause the person to burn out or cause you to give up restraining him or her. When stymied, fire types can become morose and despondent.

Fiery-type tennis pros, in the heat of the moment, toss rackets on the ground, jump around, and scream. Fire types like to be daring and will dress to attract attention. Antics notwithstanding, enthusiasm helps one reach the top in a sport. Fire types make fierce competitors.

Fire types prowl the realm of the intellect. Logic, abstractions, and synthesis of disparate concepts are intriguing to fire types. Feed them with knowledge and challenge them to defend it. When conversation seems to be thinning, ask them for their opinion on a hot topic.

A fire type is a natural salesperson. The product is not important, for a fire person really sells inspiration and the product is just a vehicle for getting your attention. Fire types need space and lots of it. Clutter makes them irritable. Their challenging characteristics tend to be exaggerated when they live with a great deal of furnishings in small spaces.

CHARACTERISTIC CHOICES OF FIRE TYPES

Fire types tend to like eclectic, bright environments. Preferring a mélange of furniture both fanciful and austere and a range of art that could include winged angels or Egyptian pyramids, their decor typically engages and entertains. It is fun to be in the home of a fire person. They give away as easily as they collect and tend to break things because they move around so quickly. Since fire is not an element but a catalyst, it is like the kind of sound that inspires or is at the epicenter of a musical arrangement. Fire persons like music with a definitive beat, tall sculptures, totems, pedestals for displaying objects, and hanging plants.

In life, fire types are most content when a job entails dealing with the unknown. Don't expect fire types to be happy on an assembly line or in a typing pool. Fire types like the limelight and are not uncomfortable in tense situations. Until they mature they tend to put their foot in their mouth, but once they mellow they make good politicians because they can respond quickly. Fire types do best with projects that have a definite end. Brainstorming sessions are more to their liking than long-term projects that have microscopic discernible results. Therefore, they are not temperamentally suited to be strategy analysts or mediators but do well as event planners and talk show hosts, all situations requiring immediate responses and garnering immediate results. Intellectual pursuits delight fire types because using their minds gives them great satisfaction. Need a strategist? Use a fire person. If you are planning a trip, let a fire person map out the route. In a world that requires quick responses because there are so many decisions to make, fire types are likely to thrive.

COMBINATIONS OF THE ESSENTIAL NATURE OF FIRE

Expressed Fire/Hidden Fire Type

 Step aside! Nothing and no one stops a double fire. Quick to become enraged and engaged, double-fire types delight in absorbing volumes of information, synthesizing it, and spewing it out in another form. At a board table they are the ones to readily accept a challenge, can come up with ideas, and can discard old, ineffective practices with ease. With only the impetus to alter situations, fire/fire types can be demanding and infuriating to live with. On the bright side, they can add drama and excitement with their enthusiasm. If you need someone present and available for you all the time, don't choose a double fire, but if you want to be with a person who stimulates you and spurs you on to investigate anything and everything, a double-fire type is ideal.

What Expressed Fire/Hidden Fire Types Need in Their Space
Fire/fire types need lots of grounded earth elements in their space—tables with bases as opposed to legs, beds with skirts to the floor, and cabinets with drawers to the floor. Before you introduce a sensitive topic or expect an intimate response with a double fire, consider carefully where you sit and what you wear. Do not face the fire/fire person toward a door, for he or she will want to exit, if only mentally, during any stressful conversation. Do not wear bright colors or bold prints, because the fire/fire person can be distracted by bold prints and vivid colors, which typically engage and energize, something a fire doesn't usually need anymore of. If you have a water feature in your home, sit close to it. If not, sit around a square table or across a diagonal to the fire/fire type. Do not sit side by side or directly across from a double-fire type if you want to have a glimmer of hope of them focusing.

Expressed Fire/Hidden Earth Type

A fire/earth combination, while needing others, is not dependent on them. A fire/earth person might be emotionally unavailable for a stretch but will be able to connect deeply when focused on doing so. Fire/earth types make excellent parents and lovers too. This combination needs to relax more physically and emotionally than other fire types. Although fire/earth types make far too many plans and assume too much responsibility, they usually accomplish what they set out to do.

While desiring to be free to do what they choose, fire/earth people desperately want to avoid isolation. They love to travel and are apt to wait until they have enough money to go in style. While being able to see a whole picture, they can understand the detailed process of making a function, organization, or relationship work.

Combining both compassion and loyalty, fire/earth types don't tend to stray, especially when their environment contains lots of water elements.

What Expressed Fire/Hidden Earth Types Need in Their Space
Strategically placed, water's colors, blue or black, can help fire/earth types get in touch with their emotional needs. Although they typically prefer solid fabrics, some accessories such as throw pillows, dinner plates, and bedsheets should have water's undulating lines. A splash of sunflower yellow in an out-of-the-way location can help them pause long enough to connect to their feelings. A poster with large areas of yellow mounted in a home's entrance, a yellow birdhouse hung outside a bathroom window, and a yellow mug for a morning brew are a few disarming ways to infuse yellow.

If you want to woo a fire/earth type, bring him or her red blooming plants such as poinsettias for every Christmas. Begonias with a bottle of wine, or roses and chocolates can reinforce their fire/earth qualities and hence be especially affirming.

Expressed Fire/Hidden Metal Type

A fire/metal person is hard to hold down and restrain from latching on to new ideas or becoming extremely involved with the latest trend. Anyone who tries can be scorched. If you want a mate who is ready to do what you want, don't choose a fire/metal person. They are self-starters and typically are very involved in their work or leisure activities. If you are in a relationship with a fire/metal type, develop other interests or align yourself with your partner's rather than becoming frustrated trying to seduce him or her to follow you.

Fire/metal people combine charisma with self-righteousness. Able to pare ideas down to their essence, fire/metal types have the ability to convince others of what they know intuitively. If not duplicitous, their intimate relationships tend to be straightforward, moral, and exciting. If they tend to fabricate, watch out. They can spin a yarn longer than the road to Mandalay, and you won't doubt for a moment its authenticity.

What Expressed Fire/Hidden Metal Types Need in Their Space

Add earth and water to their environment and stay away from wood. Light to medium sand colors are better than deeper ones because they like clarity, which dark places don't support. Trim woodwork around a window with a sand or yellow tone to help them stay emotionally connected to home. Fire/metal types like surprises and need complex spaces. No blank walls for them anywhere. Be sure the bathroom they use has artwork on the walls, and it's not a bad idea to have a small bookshelf holding magazines and newspapers to read. These types like fodder for thought all around. Comfort is critical for these people, because it's the only way to keep them seated for any period of time.

Expressed Fire/Hidden Water Type

 Fire and water can put themselves out. Although their outward demeanor seems too optimistic to be seriously altered, their enthusiasm can be washed away rather quickly by adversity. On one hand that quality can serve them well, such as when a goal cannot be reached, for fire/water types can turn on a dime and find another interest to throw their hardworking selves into. On the other hand, rather minor setbacks sometimes throw them off track.

Fire/water types will not alter their feelings slowly over time. They are likely to stay involved until the limit of their patience is reached and then rapidly depart from a negative situation. This combination thrives on showing you how to cut a carrot or tie a sailor's knot. They adore demonstrating what they love and know.

A fire/water partner can live with many different types and collect a whole array of disparate friends. Having two catalysts in their makeup, they are able to be all things to all people. While they do not necessarily appear to listen, they can be counted on for understanding as well as motivation.

What Expressed Fire/Hidden Water Types Need in Their Space

Security is primary for this combination. Needing sufficient room to move around at home, these people must not have too many objects or clutter. No wobbly tables or flimsy pedestals for them. Heavy carved wooden-legged tables and marble tops are just right as is nonglare glass. Oils, bas-relief, handmade paper sculpture, and macramé are the sorts of items good to position in full view near their favorite seating spot. If they don't have a favorite seat, place these sorts of items across from their chair at the dining room table.

Expressed Fire/Hidden Wood Type

 Understand that fire/wood types can express one thing and mean another. Since both their fire and wood elements want to get through a discussion, strategy meeting, or difficult situation, they tend to dismiss feelings and may appear to be insensitive to others' emotional needs. Fire/wood types don't like the therapeutic process; they prefer to seize solutions and change promptly.

When problems need to be worked out, start from scratch. Don't move on to the next point until you have secured their acceptance. It is important to start anew if something doesn't feel right. Since fire/wood people are extremely interested in results, if all else fails they will try to secure power and bring about a resolution by dominating a situation. This is a tough combination to argue with.

Be willing to move, change jobs, test out new hobbies, and risk safety for excitement. Fire/wood types can be ardent supporters of unusual causes and will likely back your dreams too.

What Expressed Fire/Hidden Wood Types Need in Their Space

While you don't want to extinguish their enthusiasm, you do want to slow them down. Dark flooring can help fire/wood types focus on emotional needs while not extinguishing their enthusiasm. Charcoal tiles, medium-gray carpet, or area rugs with blue or black are ideal. Another unique way to add the water element to their flooring is by selecting a ceramic floor tile with a variegated texture or a carpet with twisted fibers. Sculpted Italian modern furniture with its undulating shapes, Victorian rounded sofas and cabinets, curved chairs, headboards, and picture or mirror frames are all good to place in a fire/wood's environment.

Balancing the Fire Person

Earth balances fire in the least intrusive manner. Metal controls fire. Water can control or restrain fire. Wood can be destroyed by fire, and earth can balance it. The following descriptions can help you understand the full impact of each element on fire. Not all elements need balancing all the time. Sometimes the full impact of an element's natural proclivity is appropriate for a situation.

Balancing Fire by Adding Fire

Believe it or not, there are times when you have to fight fire with fire. When all else fails to calm or reduce a fire's blaze, add more fire elements to the home. It can be like a slap in the face to a hysterical person. Be prepared to sizzle, and then help your fire type regain composure. First, however, try one of the other elements for balance.

Balancing Fire by Adding Earth

Earth is a good balance for fire types. It gives them a secure base from which to spring and prevents them from being scorched by the heat their activities generate. If you're not the earth type yourself and want to provide a safe haven for a fire type, add earth elements like red terra-cotta planters; square lamp shades; beige, brown, or tan fabrics; and chunky, firm, squat furniture. Wood-colored vertical blinds or valances on windows, fabrics or rugs with squares, and brown wooden parquet floors can relax a fire type. Earth reduces fire's characteristics in a gentle, nonintrusive way, just as dirt covering a campfire will quietly smother it. Stay away from shiny, polished surfaces and slick, smooth fabrics.

A fire person who suffers from anxiety or phobias will find it comforting to be around an earth type. When learning new skills an earth instructor can help a fire type to relax and focus.

Balancing Fire by Adding Metal

Metal takes some heat from fire. Mutable, excitable fire persons can become calm with metal. Fire types can think over their ideas or actions with more equanimity when metal is in their environment. Nonshiny metal surfaces are better to select than shiny ones because dull metal will encourage action without speeding up the mental process.

A fire person who lives in a space with a great deal of glossy surfaces and mirrors may, however, find himself becoming enervated. With too much metal, fire types can be sapped of their verve, curiosity and natural optimism. Reduce the element metal in an environment when a fire type exhibits nervous habits such as nail biting.

Balancing Fire by Adding Water

When water elements fill a space, expect fire types to become less volatile, then edgy, and finally overwhelmed. Water can extinguish a blaze, as can a water partner help an out-of-control fire person calm down. When the challenged fire characteristics are in disproportion to the positive ones, adding water elements to a home can help to reverse them. In cases when the challenging aspects of fire are out of control, try dumping some water elements into a dining, TV, or reading room. That's if you can get your fire person to sit down long enough to feel the tranquilizing effect of water.

Introducing a small, intense water element like an area rug or throw pillow can help fire buckle down to work. For example, I have a fire-type friend who hates to make telephone calls. To help him focus, I suggested he purchase a blue phone. His anxiety can be somewhat calmed by his observing a dab of water's color, blue.

Balancing Fire by Adding Wood

The element wood is often incorrectly only associated with the material wood. Wood's color is green, while real wood is more of an earth color. Don't surround fire types with a great deal of wood elements unless you can stand the heat. Don't expect a fire type to spend a great deal of time at home or in a room filled with the color green, the color associated with the wood element. Fire types are likely to double their pace and put forth enormous energy in an environment with many wood elements. In fact fire works especially well in a wood office and can be a good business partner with wood. What works in a work space, though, may not be as beneficial in a residence.

Fire types feel frustrated and scornful with those who are content to merely talk about a situation rather than take action to change it. In general fire types like to have some wood in their spaces so they can spend some of their boundless energy.

Best Partners for Fire

If you are . . .	Your best partnership combination is . . .
fire/fire	wood/earth or earth/wood, earth/earth
fire/earth	earth/water
fire/metal	earth/earth
fire/water	earth/metal
fire/wood	earth/water
earth/fire	fire/earth, water/metal
metal/fire	water/earth
water/fire	metal/earth
wood/fire	water/earth

Challenging Partners for Fire

If you are . . .	Your challenging partnership combination is . . .
fire/fire	water/metal or metal/water, fire/water or water/fire
fire/earth	metal/water
fire/metal	water/wood, wood/fire, metal/fire
fire/water	water/fire, earth/earth
fire/wood	fire/metal, metal/metal, wood/metal, water/metal
earth/fire	wood/metal, water/water
metal/fire	wood/water
water/fire	fire/fire, fire/water
wood/fire	fire/metal

PARTNERS FOR FIRE

The following measures can help balance fire's partnerships.

Fire as Fire's Partner

Fire types living together are dynamic, active, and if not restrained by having water or earth elements at home can overload and self-destruct. Friends can find it almost unbearable to be with a fire-fire partnership for long periods of time because their nonstop energy can be exhausting.

Double-fire couples need to surround themselves with deep blues, blacks, and grays, not greens, whites, and oranges. It is best to have mostly solid fabrics, for too many lines are distracting for this energetic pair. Full-spectrum lights are far better than incandescent because they have in their illuminations all colors. Double fires need an array of tones rather than a monochromatic scheme.

Earth as Fire's Partner

Earth is a great combination with fire so long as the earth person is not prone to depression or stagnation. If so, the fire partner will become frustrated and bored. When a person's earth characteristics are positive, earth allows fire the freedom to be itself and not burn out. Earth types find life enriching with fire.

If you are trying to attract a fire person and are a strong earth type, be sure to have a few mirrors. Cover pictures with reflective instead of nonglare glass. Fire types need both some stimulation and something to absorb their heat. Metal will do both. When you introduce brass, chrome, silver, or gold, the ambience will enhance the more reserved qualities of earth to satisfy fire's desire for excitement.

Metal as Fire's Partner

Since metal reacts to fire, life will be interesting and stimulating for a fire/metal partnership. When a fire and a metal type are partners, adding earth or water to their setting will do much to calm the atmosphere. However, if fire is the stronger partner, a metal person may feel irritated by fire's need for attention. If life gets too boring or calm for the fire partner, add wood—lots of green plants, striped fabrics, vertical blinds, floor lamps, columns, and tables with legs instead of pedestals. Wood elements distract fire and will give metal types the freedom to do their own thing.

Water as Fire's Partner

Water and fire do not make a natural combination, for they can sabotage each other's natural tendencies. For a fire type and a water type to coexist, add a great deal of earth with a dash of metal as a stimulant. Home should be filled with colors like marigold, pansy violet, burnished orange, and chocolate brown and accented with gold, copper, and bronze picture frames, lighting fixtures, and doorknobs.

Wood as Fire's Partner

Fire types love wood types, for wood stimulation satisfies fire's appetite for excitement. When the fire partner is the stronger partner, the wood partner may lose enthusiasm for the relationship because fire has a tendency to want to control wood. A strong wood person, however, even a double wood, is capable of holding his or her own. Add items with luster such as mother-of-pearl or tortoiseshell to give each partner a feeling of autonomy. Unusual items such as chairs made from horns, collections of brass instruments, and boxes of inlaid materials can be a perfect foil, for a metal-earth combination in an environment benefits a wood/fire partnership.

10

EARTH TYPE

Shape: square—associated with the feeling of stability as is the earth

Color: terra-cotta—associated with the color of the soil in your area

Texture: firm—associated with the feeling of standing on the ground

Direction: center—as the earth's surface is the epicenter of our lives

Smell/Taste: floral/musk/sweet—the aroma of healthy, fresh soil

Sound: drums—like a heartbeat

Season: May/Sept.—the central times of the year when changes begin to unfold

Positive Characteristics of Earth

steadfast
loyal
consistent
realistic
exploring

family and community oriented
peacemaking
calm

Challenging Characteristics of Earth

stubborn
risk averse
resistant to new ideas or trends or exploration
uncomfortable with change
greedy
manipulating

Partner Who Controls Earth

wood, water

Partner Who Balances Earth

earth, metal

Partner Who Supports Earth

fire

Partner Who Is Supported by Earth

metal, wood

Partner Who Is Restrained by Earth

water

OVERVIEW

Are you considered the Rock of Gibraltar? Do others seek your advice and count on you to be a voice of reason and moderation? Earth types enjoy vacationing in one location and exploring deeply rather than visiting five cities in seven days. Earth persons are good at making others feel secure and grounded and can be counted on to be there when needed. When in trouble or anxious, seek the company of an earth person.

On the other hand, a challenged earth person can be so stuck in protocol that all forests are obscured by the trees. For those who fling themselves into the fray of life, living with an earth person can be the tether that holds them safely in place. On the challenging side, an earth person will not want to assume risk or will talk a loved one out of risk taking. Challenged earth types do not like changing careers, partners, or furniture.

My friends Sandy and Ted have collected art for more than thirty years. Their purchases are made without premeditation, and they never know when they are going to find something they have to have. Although their collection ranges from primitive to sophisticated and from antique to contemporary, the shapes are all chunky and squat but whimsical. In some ways these seemingly disparate concepts reflect perfectly the prevailing theme of their lives. As their choices display, both are magical but trapped under thick layers of resistance. This is a dichotomy of the element earth: one aspect stuck like a stubborn bureaucrat, the other aspect freely mobile like topsoil carried downstream by the melting mountain snows.

Know that overall earth types like repetition. They are not bored by reading a book a second time or seeing a beloved movie over and over again. How far they are likely to roam or how much they will risk is a function of the other elements in their makeup. The earth element stays put when nothing intrudes on it.

Able to accept a role assigned to them, earth types are polite and loyal and tend to keep up with correspondence and old friends. Count on them to do what they say, because they want to please and are adverse to being without attachments. Good at details but resistant to interference, earth people can be counted on to finish a job if they don't collapse from assuming too much responsibility before the job is completed.

CHARACTERISTIC CHOICES OF EARTH TYPES

Earth's materials are fairly obvious; they include pottery, dishes, glass (which is made with sand and water), concrete, and bricks. Earth colors can be brown, sand, reddish, or whatever color reflects an area's soil. Earth types tend to choose chunky, solid objects and typically have three-dimensional artifacts.

Earth types love to have direct contact with materials and be in a position to maintain rather than initiate. Gardening, working with clay, baking bread, or being a hockey team's goalie feels more comfortable than swimming, carpentry, or playing tight end on a football team. They are not uncomfortable with taking a long time to complete projects and persist long after others abandon them.

One way to tell if a person has some challenging characteristics is to notice how many items are located near the home's front entrance. Challenged earth people typically crowd things near doorways, as if filling up a hole.

THE ESSENTIAL NATURE OF EARTH

Expressed Earth/Hidden Fire Type

A person with an earth personality and fire emotions can be hard to figure out. A stoic exterior belies what's underneath. Apt to have a wry sense of humor, this combination might appear quiet but rarely is. Just like a raging fire at the earth's center, what's going on emotionally in an earth/fire type is often unknowable. Earth people serve best as powers behind the throne and make superb assistants. Steady, dependable, with a straightforward approach, earth/fire types can be remarkably innovative and, when brainstorming, often come up with the perfect concept.

Julie moved from Chicago to Florida when her husband was transferred. Upbeat, optimistic, and filled to the brim with energy, she began a job search soon after the transfer. I interviewed Julie one evening after returning from a long, tiring trip. Wearing a sedate outfit and quelling her natural enthusiasm, she did not strike me as a fire type. In fact I thought she possessed too much earth for the position. Boy, was I wrong! When she arrived and was able to feel comfortable with her surroundings, her hidden fire ignited. Having the capacity to make even the most incendiary situation calm, she also has a hidden vitality that helps me keep my hectic work-related life in optimum working order.

Needing to feel connected to a place, person, or situation, those with expressed earth and hidden fire are attached to and protective of those they love. Once they count you among their friends, you can count on them to be loyal and indefatigable.

What Expressed Earth/Hidden Fire Types Need in Their Space

To release their fiery spirit, add metal to an environment. Reflective frames for artwork and strategically placed mirrors and dishes with silver or gold trim will help earth/fires be more expressive.

Flute music, candlelight, and deeply aromatic floral fragrances at dinner can be a catalyst to ignite emotional fire. Stay away from the water element in an environment. It can drown their internal fire and stifle their ability to be verbally expressive.

If someone with this combination tends to be easily angered or is at a volatile time in life, stay away from using too much green. Wood's green color can exacerbate negativity. It is appropriate during these periods to purchase blue or black for items used sparingly such as dinner napkins or pillowcases. Water's color will help to cool down extreme emotions.

Expressed Earth/Hidden Earth Type

 When a double earth doesn't like something, it's almost impossible to reverse his or her opinion. But if you need someone who will always be there for you, choose this type. Once committed to a person or a project, an earth person will see it through to the end, no matter what. While consistency can be an endearing quality, being a double earth can push this trait over to inflexibility, especially if you are free-spirited.

Double-earth types abhor having to divide their loyalties and find the pull between career and home frustrating. They absolutely want to be married and will avoid isolation at all costs. Don't play hard to get with an earth/earth type.

What Expressed Earth/Hidden Earth Types Need in Their Space

Water seeks the lowest ground and will ultimately move mountains. Adding water's colors or shapes to this type's bedroom, bathroom, or kitchen can, over the long haul, be the catalyst that shakes the person out of inflexibility. Do not, however, use water alone. Metal should be added along with water. When pressure is exerted on earth, it forms materials like gold, silver, and copper. When earth people have metal's mandate in an environment they can often focus and pay attention to their unique talents. Therefore, furniture with rounded edges, area carpets in lieu of wall-to-wall carpeting, and textured wallpaper or fabrics in salmons, grays, or mustard can do the trick. When earth/earth types need a big push to change, add fire and lots of it. Red candlesticks, throw pillows, or a red Oriental carpet is ideal.

Expressed Earth/Hidden Metal Type

A treasure is hidden within earth/metal types, for whatever they express outwardly they have refined inside. Many of my friends who sail are this type. Earth/metals don't get befuddled in a crisis but can stay calm and think clearly. Earth/metal finds problem solving easy and thrives in challenging situations. Long-term projects and goals that require a great deal of patience to achieve are ideal for earth/metal, for this type does not need to be gratified immediately.

While earth/metal people do not covet a leadership role, they are not inclined to follow. It is easy for this combination to see both sides of a conflict, so they can be good mediators. Although not likely to jump on the bandwagon of new ideas, they are also not likely to reject them. It may appear to you that they are indecisive, not always having a firmly entrenched viewpoint, but don't let that fool you. These types tend to be loyal and possess deeply thought out but not necessarily articulated viewpoints.

Earth/metal types are inclined to do civic work and tend to be involved in environmental issues. If you are looking for a partner to debate the cosmos with, look elsewhere. Desiring harmony, they are intent on dealing with the here and now more than on what might be.

To woo an earth/metal type, surprise him or her by planning getaway weekends in isolated areas. This type loves spontaneity and hates crowds.

What Expressed Earth/Hidden Metal Types Need in Their Space

Moderate stimulation—lots of movement, plants, and pets—will keep earth/metal types from being bored. Bonsai trees or plants that can be trained across a horizontal plane or air ducts aimed at plants are good ways to add movement. Paddle fans, a bell attached to their study's doorknob, and lamps that can be turned on by hand claps add physical interaction and are other ways to keep them engaged.

Expressed Earth/Hidden Water Type

While they might not show it, the emotions of earth/water types run deep. Brace yourself when their emotions come rolling ashore, for like a tidal wave, their feelings are intense and sometimes uncontrollable. The problem for earth/water types is to find a way to express these feelings appropriately. Often earth/water types are not talkative and find conversation and verbal communication difficult, which means if you want to unearth their feelings you should be prepared to probe.

If you want someone who will unravel the mysteries of the cosmos or will be a personal mentor, select an earth/water partner. Don't tell this person a partial secret, for earth/water types are fascinated by details and will pester you until all is revealed. They love to be relied on but like to feel protected as well. It matters little if you only protect them from the rain by having a large umbrella. Show them in as many ways as possible that you can shield them from harm and at the same time crave their attention.

What Expressed Earth/Hidden Water Types Need in Their Space

Metal is the perfect complement to this type's environment, for metal helps the ideas flow and transforms amorphous emotions into words. Metal can be like a rod, drilling deep into the earth's core to extract precious ore, and will stimulate conversation and ideas. Instead of wrought-iron or pewter accessories, select shiny metallic surfaces to install in an earth/water's environment. Shiny objects telegraph the metal element quickly and efficiently.

Wood is also a nurturing element for earth/water types, for they can be emotionally clogged and need a divining rod to help locate and define emotional needs. Place wood elements close to the ground to help them give shape to their emotional life. Plants positioned on the floor and striped fabrics on footstools, throw pillows, and area carpets are some good choices.

Expressed Earth/Hidden Wood Type

Teachers love earth/wood because they are usually easy to handle and have a penchant for learning. Earth/wood types tend to stay in the background rather than call attention to themselves; therefore their deep capacity for learning often is, at first, unnoticed. Good team players, the challenge for earth/wood is to find a unique way to relate. With their emotional life pushing them to change and their earth persona trying to keep things the same, an earth/wood type may feel stressed by contradictory impulses. Rarely asking for guidance, they tend to focus on what they can do to improve their lives and may feel unsupported by a lack of interest from others. Query earth/wood types about their job, family, and interests, and you might be surprised by how much they will reveal.

Earth/woods prefer to be able to handle whatever comes their way and don't like to display weaknesses. The more you encourage them to talk about their life, the more they will notice you.

What Expressed Earth/Hidden Wood Types Need in Their Space

A home filled with metal shapes and colors replenishes an earth/wood type. Focus on the most private areas, such as a bathroom, study, or bedroom. Dotted bedsheets, silver and gold shower curtains, gold faucet fixtures, silver inkwells and pen holders, brass desk lamps, mirrors, metallic picture frames, and gold-trimmed phones are some smaller items that represent the metal element.

Water is another element that when used below chest height will add the right nourishment to an earth/wood's environment. Place black items on a desktop such as black-encased computer screens, paper clip holders, phones, cellophane tape holder, Rolodexes, horizontal black file cabinets, fax machines, desks, and low cabinets. Avoid black lighting fixtures, frames for wall art, and window treatments and vertical black file cabinets.

BALANCING THE EARTH PERSON

Expressed or hidden earth can be balanced by the following alterations to the environment.

Balancing Earth by Adding Fire

When an earth type is stuck in a rut or needs inspiration, introduce any fire element, but mostly its shape, the triangle. Like an erupting volcano spewing earth, adding fabrics with triangular patterns can dissipate negativity or a bad habit. Earth folks are the only ones who can live with burgundy or red wall coverings. In fact, using red accents on walls will produce a stronger sense of personal worth for earth types.

Balancing Earth by Adding Earth

Get ready to go nowhere. Earth/earth will not take chances with careers, relationships, or travel. Adding additional earth elements to the environment of an earth person will render him or her immobile. Even the healthiest earth types can, when there is an abundance of earth colors and shapes, become dogmatic and headstrong. Increasing the earth during a life crisis or exceptionally stressful time is the single exception.

Balancing Earth by Adding Metal

When it's time for an earth person to make a decision, add metal. Metal helps earth to solidify ideas. To stimulate an earth to make a decision, use wrought-iron or verdigris candlesticks or a silver vase filled with white gardenias or roses. To help an earth type become more flexible, add metal's reflective quality and keep the room temperature a few degrees cooler than it presently is.

Balancing Earth by Adding Water

Mix water with earth and you have a substance that can be moved, poured, and shaped. Earth persons do well with water elements in their homes.

For the most part water and earth change slowly, unless there is a catastrophe. Tidal waves or earthquakes can cause water and earth to become raging monsters, but this happens only when conditions are extreme. Earth types are slow to be provoked, but if you exceed acceptable boundaries, expect a monumental reaction. If an earth type becomes angry or appears to be suffering from the effects of stress, keep an extra dose of a water element nearby. In an emergency, buy blue bedsheets or ones with wavy-lined prints. Cover a dining table with a blue cloth or buy blue paper towels, tissue, toilet paper, and table napkins.

Since water is a force that can move mountains over time, use water to help an inflexible earth type shift. Water assists in transforming reluctance into acceptance. Water can shift, blend, or overwhelm earth; the secret lies in the amount and form used.

When there are no salient problems, keep the ratio of water to earth at one to three. Balance a square dining room table with gold and burnt-orange checked fabric on low straight-backed chairs with lilacs filling a black onyx hourglass-shaped vase. A little water can do wonders to balance an earth person.

Balancing Earth by Adding Wood

Earth people love plants and often are involved in landscaping or gardening. However, inside their home the wood element saps them of energy in the same way as vegetation sucks nutrients from the soil. If they have decorated their homes with a great deal of green, they may be feeling overwhelmed or enervated. With too much wood element, earth can be rendered immobile.

If actual wood or the color green is preferred, be sure it is raised from the floor—for example, a wood cornice or pictures with a great deal of green.

Best Partners for Earth

If you are . . .	Your best partnership combination is . . .
earth/fire	fire/metal, metal/earth
earth/earth	metal/fire or fire/metal, metal/water
earth/metal	fire/earth, fire/water, earth/water
earth/water	metal/metal
earth/wood	metal/earth or earth/metal, metal/water, fire/water, fire/earth
fire/earth	earth/fire
metal/earth	fire/metal, water/fire
water/earth	wood/water, wood/metal
wood/earth	water/fire, earth/fire

Rectangles in furniture, artwork, and floral arrangements are good ways to add the wood element to an earth's environment.

Challenging Partners for Earth

If you are . . .	*Your challenging partnership combination is . . .*
earth/fire	water/earth, wood/water, earth/earth, water/metal
earth/earth	water/wood or wood/water
earth/metal	wood/wood, wood/fire
earth/water	wood/fire, water/water
earth/wood	water/fire
fire/earth	water/water, water/wood
metal/earth	wood/water
water/earth	earth/wood, fire/metal
wood/earth	fire/water, metal/water

PARTNERS FOR EARTH

The following measures can help balance earth's partnerships.

Fire as Earth's Partner

Earth will typically be dazzled by a fiery partner, and if a fire person is not too competitive, earth can enjoy the sizzle. Fire and earth types like very different colors, textures, and art, and it is best to let the earth person select the upholstery pieces and the fire type to select the wall art. Since earth tends to spend more time at home, seating units should resonate with the earth person's needs. On the other hand, fire types rarely sit still, and as they move around the home the wall art is more within their field of vision.

Fire types find themselves easily seduced by earth's steadfastness but may be bored after the novelty fades or just frustrated by earth's more sober characteristics. To ensure that doesn't happen, have more fire elements in the environment than others. Rust flooring, picture frames with red lines set on gold, and mahogany trim are some modest ways fire's color, red, can be introduced to incite earth to physical or emotional action.

While fire people seek excitement, earth types seek consistency. These two make compatible bedfellows only when both are mature. If a fire person has not sown his or her wild oats or is much younger than the earth, this can be a difficult partnership.

Earth as Earth's Partner

Typically two earth types merely tolerate being together unless they think, believe, and act in markedly similar ways. To blossom, the double-earth partnership might need to add stimulation. A dazzling array of objects, lots of movement, and a prodigious amount of patterns are just fine for a double-earth partnership. Two earths might need duplicate computers to foster optimum stimulation. Bright lighting is imperative, because earth types tend to have a very yin atmosphere, which exacerbates being sedentary. Without bright colors and adequate lighting two earths might find themselves packing on the pounds. If security and steadfastness are prime attractions for both, then a double-earth combination can be successful.

Metal as Earth's Partner

Metal's characteristics usually represent what earth types wish to be. Earth often admires metal types, and if the metal partner is flexible he or she can help the earth person transform dreams into reality. The key ingredient for the metal partner is patience.

Water as Earth's Partner

Water types can assist earth to take action. However, an earth person who is fiercely independent might resent water's persistence. Normally water can be sensitive and responsive and have the patience to wait for an earth partner to make up his or her mind or change. Water's ability to communicate can provide earth with the confidence to open up and let a water partner infiltrate his or her psyche.

Water types like cool, moist surroundings and are more interested in the end product or overall feel than the details. Water is more content spending time shopping for exotic foods and preparing a gourmet meal than eating meals in nondescript restaurants. This enthralls earth, for earth types love to spend time at home.

Water tends to engage in more activities than an earth person, but all in all this combination makes for a good partnership. If you are a water type, you will find the pace and stamina of earth comforting. Earth should be aware that water types might conceal things from them instead of being challenged to provide lengthy explanations.

Wood as Earth's Partner

Wood types want others to be able to change effortlessly, which is difficult for earth types to do. Those with wood dominating find it natural to move from place to place and can exert pressure on an earth partner to do the same. While earth types find change intriguing, they can be somewhat puzzled by a wood type's desire to keep changing even when a situation is satisfactory. A wood person whose elemental chart has a touch of water or earth will find partnering with earth less frustrating.

Earth loves watching wood rally around causes and can keep wood types on course and not become too overcommitted. While wood likes to expand and avoid being held back, earth can hold down the fort and keep the home fires burning if only metaphorically. Wood types need earth but are stingy in showing their appreciation.

11

METAL TYPE

Shape: round—when metal contracts, it forms a ball

Color: white, gold, silver, copper—reflective colors

Texture: smooth—as are the surfaces of metal when formed or heated

Direction: west—direction of the setting sun or endings, constrictions like metal when shaped with heat

Smell/Taste: acrid—the scent of burning metal

Sound: xylophone, piano—uses metal strings to resonate tones

Season: fall—metal is the end result of earth's pressure, and harvest is at fall's end

Positive Characteristics of Metal

thorough
curious
focused
discerning
serious
refined
analytical

Challenging Characteristics of Metal

defensive
withdrawn

arrogant
picky
constraining
emotionally unavailable

Partner Who Controls Metal

fire

Partner Who Balances Metal

water

Partner Who Supports Metal

earth

Partner Who Is Supported by Metal

water

Partner Who Is Restrained by Metal

wood

OVERVIEW

Metal types love to distill things to their essence, removing what is impure and superfluous. Editors who are metal types thrive on paring down manuscripts. Solving puzzles and riddles thrills them. Metal types like to gather information and shape ideas. If you are courting a metal person, don't pepper a conversation with off-the-cuff remarks. Metal types will review what you say and punch holes in anything not thought out carefully.

Metal's natural inclination is to remember and think about the smallest detail. Metal types feel compelled to expose truth as it is perceived and seek to know the unknowable. When not engaged in mental activities, they usually are involved with physical accomplishments. Metal types are often at the confluence of athletic prowess and mental agility and are probably the elemental combinations of many great athletes of our time and those who have overcome tremendous odds to achieve a goal. Metal types have the power to focus and control their impulses. If you want to make metal types feel good, play board or card games where they can show off their mental agility.

Albert Einstein was probably a metal type. He valued mental activities above all. Have you ever heard anything about Einstein's children and two marriages? When mental activities take precedence in life, one tends to ignore emotions. A person with too much metal does not focus on family life.

Give a metal person a goal, a deadline or an ultimatum, and he or she will meet it. Metal types feel more comfortable with time limits and boundaries than without them. This is the person in a group who can make a quick decision about which movie to see or which hospital to go to in an emergency. While striving for the highest standards for themselves, they expect all around them to do the same. Want to annoy a metal type? Do a sloppy job. Want to win over a metal type? Prepare a fabulous meal from soup to nuts.

This is not the type that appreciates practical gifts. Instead, find extravagant accessories like sterling butter knives or an obscure book of poetry. The gift of a Steuben glass vase or an exquisite rose is ideal for a metal person because he or she favors perfection. Before giving a metal type a gift, be sure to research the item thoroughly. Attention to details is high on the list of this person's priorities.

Metals hate feeling cold, so be sure your home is heated to their satisfaction.

CHARACTERISTIC CHOICES OF METAL TYPES

When metal types have a choice, they will select an object that stands out because of its unusual shape, size, shine, or subject matter. The more reflective a surface, the more stimulating it is for metal types. Circles, dots, portholes, and round columns represent metal as does a room with all white upholstery and carpeting.

Metal persons are fascinated with objects that can move. It is not unusual to find flags, windsocks, chimes, or whirligigs outside their home and music boxes with moving figurines, fans, cuckoo clocks, mobiles, and three-dimensional artifacts that move by electricity or air currents inside. Metal persons prefer to dine in a room with billowing curtains and dramatic piano music.

Most contemporary Western settings have far too much metal—a plethora of gadgets requiring electricity such as televisions, computers, stereos, radios, dishwashers, stoves, refrigerators, blenders, coffee-makers, can openers, and bread machines, even before you count items such as pots, pans, brass, silver, or chrome objects, and the colors white, silver, gold, and copper. More likely than not, the metal element should be reduced in most spaces rather than added.

THE ESSENTIAL NATURE OF METAL

Expressed Metal/Hidden Fire Type

Metal/fire types spin their wheels and jump into a project before finishing the preceding one. Loving a challenge, metal types will rarely say no if asked to help. If you want someone who can postpone personal satisfaction to get a job done, seek a metal/fire person. Give him a task and watch him go.

Metal/fire types like to be involved in adventurous vacations or ideas but cannot enjoy themselves unless they have the lion's share of responsibilities. When you want to be motivated or energized, this is the friend to call. Metal/fire people can inspire by example. They are disciplined and are not easily thwarted from realizing their goals. But beware: metal/fire types must be careful not to burn the candle at both ends. When they have taken on too much responsibility, they feel weighted down and sometimes vanish or suddenly exit a situation.

Metal/fire types suffer silently unless you are one of their inner circle of friends. If you have ever gone out with someone and had what you thought was a great time and then never heard from him or her again, most probably this was a metal/fire type. The slightest infraction can set them running, but they won't necessarily express their disapproval unless you probe. Wanting their preferences to be known, metal/fire types like to be singled out and held in regard for their individuality and mastery.

What Expressed Metal/Hidden Fire Types Need in Their Space

Metal/fire people need to have a water element in their home if they feel out of control, with too much responsibility over people, events, or paperwork. Water elements help soothe their emotions. If, however, you want them to reveal their deepest feelings, reduce the water element to a bare minimum. In the real world, water dulls metal slowly but with unwavering persistence. Therefore, the symbols of water can take the edge off metal element's natural inclination to do, to think, and to be involved sometimes in a slightly obsessive way.

If a metal/fire type's self-esteem is low or recently damaged, add wood, which is controlled by metal and augments metal/fire's self-worth. Wood-paneled libraries or studies, heavy wooden desks, or solid oak desk chairs feel comfortable for metals and can fuel their confidence.

The sounds of a water feature, slightly elevated moisture levels, and subdued lighting are ways to add water or more yin to metal/fire's scape. Since these types spend a great deal of time thinking, adding water will help lead them to their heart. If a metal/fire type needs sexual inspiration or is in the temporary doldrums, add a bit more fire in a bedroom. Red candles, a red vase, and a red flower can be just the right amount to dispel disinterest or listlessness.

Expressed Metal/Hidden Earth Type

Metal with earth inside is a complex combination. Metal people like to be authorities on a topic, and earth would rather all those involved be in accord. Sometimes this conflict is expressed by indecision, but it's the kind of indecisiveness that leaves friends dizzy because the metal personality will discuss alternatives endlessly. Metal/earth can engage in a great deal of talk before taking action. Repetition helps them feel secure. Jobs with a certain amount of redundant tasks feel comfortable for metal/earth types. Accounting, teaching, botany, personnel, crafts in any medium, and physical therapy are good choices because patience is an underlying metal/earth virtue. A metal/earth person will love to help you make decisions, write a business plan, or design a vacation. These types enjoy spending hours engaged in activities that interest them and when the subject matter thrills them can spend a whole day in a museum or reading a book. Generally faithful, they do not spread themselves too thin, preferring depth more than variety. Once a metal/earth person is committed to you, he or she will likely remain steadfast for life.

What Expressed Metal/Hidden Earth Types Need in Their Space

Fire lights this type's emotional life. To infuse enthusiasm, add burgundy colors and geometric artwork and paint an exterior door red. Eliminate too much contrast because too much opposition tends to irritate them. They have all the brightness they can stand in their expressed personality.

With all their outward intensity, it is sometimes surprising to discover that metal/earth's emotional life is often not as exciting or experimental as you might think.

When balanced and at peace with their lives, metal/earth types do best surrounded by the water element. Midtone blue and charcoal gray nubby fabrics bring fire and water together and are good choices for their interiors. Black kitchen and bathroom appliances can help them relax and give their overactive minds a rest. Metal/earth types are comfortable with endings; therefore a swivel chair facing in the direction of the setting sun is an ideal location for relaxing at the end of a day.

Expressed Metal/Hidden Metal Types

Jobs that require constant innovation and attention to detail are perfect for metal/metals, who excel as computer wizards, research scientists, and collection specialists. It's easy for double metals to verbalize ideas but not emotions. While metal/metal people can be glib and funny and explain concepts, they are not likely to be traditionally romantic. While they might spend hours finding the right birthday card or fixing your broken stereo, surprising you with a bouquet of flowers or a frivolous bauble is not likely. Never at a loss for words, whether explaining the shopping list or giving exact instructions for reaching a destination, metal/metal types have the gift of gab if they care to develop it. However, it is laborious to unearth their real feelings.

Whatever is the best quality in its category, from diamonds to Rolex watches to Rolls-Royces, is coveted by metal/metal types. Although they won't always work to make the money for these luxuries, handwoven silks, marble countertops, hand-loomed rugs, and sterling silver serving dishes thrill them. To win their hearts, surprise them by giving them a subscription to an esoteric periodical or an ounce of Russian caviar.

What Expressed Metal/Hidden Metal
Types Need in Their Space

Adding earth to an environment can help double metals slow down and focus inwardly. Using earth colors low to the ground is useless, for this type tends to look straight ahead or up. Artwork with the colors of earth, dark wood tones, and deep tawny yellows is good for clarity and grounding. Chunky rather than whimsical and leggy furniture is appreciated and enjoyed. What is seen from a favorite chair is very important since metal/metals can spend a great deal of time in one place. Since they can be distracted when facing windows, looking out on birdhouses and light-limbed trees can draw them out of their intense concentration. Repetitive movement like waves coming to shore or the soothing swaying of pine trees helps them relax. Water is a must in their scape too and should take an obvious or dominant position.

If your metal/metal person is hassled and under a great deal of pressure, add lots of earthy scents. Gardenia, ylang-ylang, patchouli, and musk are some to consider. Native drum music, pictures with bunches of yellow flowers, and a good firm back support add the earth element, which is reassuring to a double metal, especially during times of stress.

Expressed Metal/Hidden Water Type

Metal/water types bruise easily. When metal/water types say that not having been invited to an event didn't hurt their feelings, don't believe it. In fact, just the opposite is true. It is tempting to pile these people with work and give them more than their share of responsibility because they seem to be able to handle it. Seemingly tough skinned, they can take whatever is handed out for a long time but can suddenly become unnerved and come crashing down like a worn-out structural beam. Wanting to see things to completion, they will support a partner through almost any ordeal. To capture their attention, be concise. Phrase questions or information succinctly. Long-winded tirades bore them.

The way to become a metal/water's confidante is to conspire in creating a ritual. This is the type who loves anniversary dates, secret rendezvous, and a private language of allusions.

While metal/water types say they work for monetary rewards, inside they have a vision of making the world a better place. To intrigue them, speak to that hidden part. In some ways these types feel a pull to be emancipated from their internalized taskmaster and be increasingly in touch with their emotional components.

What Expressed Metal/Hidden Water
Types Need in Their Space

Use fire gingerly—just enough to convert metal from its rigid form to a more pliable substance. A desk facing south, a red pen, or artwork with accents of red are good for a work area. Fire converts obsessive thinking into action. Place red roses, red Oriental carpets, and burgundy sheets or coverlets in the bedroom to give a healthy boost to metal's sensuous side. Metal/water types are often careless with their diets. Using earth accents in the kitchen may assist them in paying attention to what they eat. Want to be noticed by a metal/water type? Wear red clothing or accessories, and when they visit keep the house dry and warm.

Be discreet in showing your affection, but definitely make a point to do so. The rigidity of metal and the fluidity of water can span the range of emotions. Metal/water is a tough combination to be, so be gentle with these types and speak to their soul more than their mind.

Expressed Metal/Hidden Wood Type

When an idea needs to be written down or a story needs telling, assign a metal/wood to the task. Likely to be writers and communicators, metal/woods have the ability to see what is happening on a gut level and translate it or articulate it so all can understand.

Metal/wood types require variety. To keep metal/woods faithful, be adventurous and innovative and by all means don't be apprehensive about showing your eccentric side. They thrive on experiencing new things and challenging themselves to excel.

This is one type where the hidden persona dominates some situations, for wood's expansive qualities can't always be contained. Metal/wood types often take up different causes during their lives. These types don't do anything halfway. Strong leaders, they demand the highest performance from those around but can be reasonable when their heart is engaged. While they often appear conforming, they admire others who dare to be different. They adore being told that you can see their uniqueness beyond their conforming exterior.

What Expressed Metal/Hidden Wood
Types Need in Their Space

Earth is a perfect complement to both metal and wood. If a metal/wood type seems restless, buy an oversized, comfortable chair, preferably one with a footrest. Only when these people are in the lap of comfort will they stay put for any length of time.

Be careful not to place them in front of a stimulating scene if you want them to listen to what you are saying. Since they tend to have active imaginations, it is easy for them to get distracted. Position them facing away from a window when dining.

Once you have a furniture arrangement that is satisfactory, don't change it often. Moving furniture in a room can exacerbate their need for personal change. Lighting should be low to the floor, so lamps are better than overhead track lighting. Dark, large-leafed plants are good so long as they are not taller than eye level when seated. Tall furniture looming near their bed or work area can make them nervous. They feel better surrounded by low dressers and credenzas. In a library, dark wooden bookcases are preferable to metal ones. Be sure to have a raised-pile welcome mat at the entrance door, which will slow them down and prevent them from slipping. Metal/wood types tend to move quickly without thought to safety.

If your metal/wood type wanders or has not committed to you, add fire to your home. A bell on a front door, a large bouquet of red blooms on the table, even twinkling Christmas lights around the perimeter of a dining room can set the stage for a romantic evening. Dazzle these people; they love it.

BALANCING THE METAL PERSON

Expressed or hidden metal can be balanced by the following alterations to the environment.

Balancing Metal by Adding Fire

Metal types will seethe when too much fire is added to an environment. Only in extreme cases, when a metal person is completely overwhelmed or worn out, is fire an appropriate element to add. Even then, be certain that any reds are muted and triangular lines are not hard edged.

Balancing Metal by Adding Earth

I suspect that all metal types love to have an earth type nourishing them. Albert Einstein's second wife was by all reports a quintessential mother earth type. She loved to cook, keep house, and generally arrange and put Einstein's physical world in order. This was perfect because metal types are not interested in nesting and can be rather indifferent toward furnishings or accessories. When they do take an interest in a home, they are likely to become interested in collecting art or artifacts, because they find it stimulating to research both the art form and the artist.

If your metal person's activities gobble up more time and energy than is healthy, adding an earth element can help him or her shed some commitments. If you are trying to snag a metal type, play music with a strong drum beat. The sound of drums grounds and relaxes these people.

Adding earth colors, boxy-shaped chairs, and lots of throw pillows is grounding and comforting to a metal type.

Balancing Metal by Adding Metal

Adding too much metal in a metal type's environment can cause both the physical environment and the person to self-destruct. Contemporary Western life is already heavily metallized, and when more metal is added the atmosphere can become too grating. *Don't* add metal in the hope of balancing metal. Only flooding the environment with water's color, shape, line, and smell has any chance of keeping a metal person sane in a home with too much metal. Purples, blues, blacks, and an assortment of fluted, dark-leafed plants can help transform an atmosphere with too many metal objects into a more satisfactory environment.

Balancing Metal by Adding Water

Water elements can balance metal, but it can take a while just as it does for water to rust metal. Patience is a virtue if you are with a metal type. If time is not a factor, adding water to a metal environment can result in long-term positive changes. Water helps to slow metal's thinking process and allows him or her the opportunity to focus deeply on one thing at a time. Use blue in small amounts, such as the background of a computer screen, cobalt-colored glasses or mugs, or a deep blue desk pad. With sufficient water, metal types become more aware of their own and others' emotional needs.

Balancing Metal by Adding Wood

Wood turns metal's thoughts into action. Wood is a counterpoint to metal in that metal's action is internal and wood's action is external. Green plants, striped wallpaper and flooring, as long as they have clean lines, can help convert metal's mental activity into accomplishments. Reed music, the throaty kind my clarinet-playing uncle Pee Wee Russell used to play, can be stimulating and sexy for metal people. Grainy textures help modify metal's intensity.

Want to get a metal type to fix something? Add wood to the space. Wood's grainy quality converts some of metal's passivity into action. Wood tempts metal to become involved.

Best Partners for Metal

If you are . . .	*Your best partnership combination is . . .*
metal/fire	earth/earth, water/earth
metal/earth	wood/water, water/fire
metal/metal	fire/water or water/fire, earth/water or water/earth, metal/metal
metal/water	wood/earth
metal/wood	earth/water, earth/earth
fire/metal	earth/wood
earth/metal	metal/earth
water/metal	wood/water
wood/metal	water/earth

Challenging Partners for Metal

If you are . . .	*Your challenging partnership combination is . . .*
metal/fire	fire/metal, fire/water
metal/earth	wood/water, earth/metal
metal/metal	wood/wood
metal/water	fire/earth, wood/water
metal/wood	wood/metal, fire/wood
fire/metal	wood/earth
earth/metal	water/wood
water/metal	fire/wood
wood/metal	metal/fire

Partners for Metal

The following measures can help balance metal's partnerships.

Fire as Metal's Partner

Fire types can surprise metal types because they appear hasty to communicate how they feel. While metal and fire may both have quick response systems, it is more likely that a fire type will reveal what is going on in his head. If you have a lover with fire, don't be daunted by his propensity to be emotionally distant or controlling. A partnership with fire can be gratifying if the metal person has some earth or fire in his or her emotional makeup. A partnership between metal and fire will not be stymied by convention or restraints. They will encourage each other to dare to do what they long for.

Earth as Metal's Partner

For metal there is nothing so supporting or affirming as living with an earth type, so long as the two are equals. Earth supports metal's unending activities, and metal appreciates earth's stabilizing power. When the metal partner is dominant, the effects are deleterious to both. Metal's intensity can engulf earth like a collar pulled too tightly around a dog's neck. If earth is dominant, metal will have a hard time climbing out from under. Earth can have a prisonlike hold over metal.

Metal as Metal's Partner

Two metals are a good combination, for both are independent and self-sufficient. Two metals with the same career can be extremely happy together and will give each other the respect and space to thrive. I suspect my editor and her husband are both metal types. Involved in the same industry, they both happily make changes in their lives for each other. If I were a fly on the wall, I probably would be privileged to hear lengthy conversations about life, children, authors, and books. Metal partners love to talk about ideas.

However, if there are areas in which there is a disagreement, metal partners can drive each other crazy. Self-righteous, they will argue until one is worn down. There is nothing worse for metal people than to be strayed from their course of action.

Water as Metal's Partner

If you are a metal type who spends too much time in your head, consider looking for a water partner. Water balances metal by helping metal feel needed. If a metal person has fears about revealing emotions, water is the best choice for a partner.

Since water types are patient, they can be perfect partners for metal types, who are usually inventive and intense. Water persons will keep sending out a metal type's résumé, entering them in contests, and applying for contestant status on game shows until they get results. Water's inner strength allows metal types to do what they do best—invent, create, and originate.

Wood as Metal's Partner

Mature, fulfilled metal persons delight in sharing a loved one's achievements. For wood that is ideal. However, challenged metal people will often feel jealous, competitive, or suspicious of a wood partner's explosive qualities, for they wish they could be less constrained and inhibited. Both fear discord, for it takes them off purpose. Both wood and metal like to listen but desire to follow a self-directed course.

12

WATER TYPE

Shape: wavy—similar to waves or the edge of water as it laps to shore

Color: black or blue—water reflects the sky or obscures light

Texture: open weave—water will flow in any direction to circumvent an obstacle

Direction: north—just as it becomes cold when light is obscured, north in our hemisphere is the direction of cold weather

Smell/Taste: ethereal—unique as well as hard to describe—like a banana

Music: harp or violin—the vibrations of unencased strings consume the air waves as water consumes its space

Season: winter—just as water prevents light and the sun's warmth from penetrating winter, winter represents the darkest, coldest months

Positive Characteristics of Water

sympathetic
flexible
loving
accommodating
compassionate
honest
insightful
self-sufficient

Challenging Characteristics of Water

overemotional
easily hurt
emotionally needy
temperamental
self-indulgent
rash
critical
secretive

Partner Who Controls Water

earth

Partner Who Balances Water

wood

Partner Who Supports Water

metal, earth

Partner Who Is Supported by Water

wood

Partner Who Is Restrained by Water

fire

OVERVIEW

Water types go with the flow and are capable of understanding both sides of an issue. They make wonderful caretakers since nurturing comes naturally to them. Usually able to make steady eye contact, water types are inclined to listen deeply and consider what is being said to them. With a tendency to be quiet, they run the risk of not being noticed by the more flamboyant types around them or in a crowd. Water types have sustained staying power, and if one is courting you, even rejection won't curtail his or her pursuit.

Not normally intimidated by adverse situations, they can overcome emotional wounds and figure out a way of dealing with situations. Too much water in a personality can, however, stifle creativity. Two water types living together can become emotionally overloaded and need to seek avenues of relief. Just as a river's bank will flood and either add nutrients to the surrounding land or destroy whatever is in its path, too much water can either be a positive or a negative contribution to life.

Keeping thoughts to themselves until they are sure of another's response, water types can be secretive and appear reserved. However, when committed, they find it hard to become unattached, so don't seek intimacy with a water type unless you are serious. You may find them stringing along after you. They are attracted to decisiveness and high energy and enraged by rapid change.

Water types are likely to be sympathetic and concerned with others' feelings. Water types tend to absorb others' elements and be absorbed by them. Since water is a catalyst, it changes most substances. If you are excitable, living with a water person will calm you. If you tend to spend too much time at work, you will be encouraged to relax.

Setting appropriate boundaries is essential because water types are naturally empathetic and can find themselves being taken advantage of. When an occasion demands, water types tend to jump in, not with the bravado of fire, the problem-solving capability of wood, the strength of metal, or the stability provided by earth, but with a sensitivity for how the outcome will affect all concerned.

CHARACTERISTIC CHOICES OF WATER TYPES

Plush fabrics, round-backed chairs and sofas, and plenty of undulating lines are typical choices of water types. Preferring low lighting, darker colors, and quiet music, female water types will welcome surprise gifts of cut flowers rather than chocolates and males will enjoy the latest magazine or book. Water types tend to crowd spaces. Having more, not less, feels better to them. They collect for the joy of having the object, not necessarily for future potential monetary rewards.

Water types can be lulled into watching too much television, and it is better not to have a TV set displayed prominently in a gathering room or bedroom. Water types love to read books by the same author and see plays by the same playwright. They will be zealous supporters of a favorite writer, actor, or director. When a water type is on your side, you have a long-term ally.

On the challenging side, water types can be self-indulgent and self-absorbed. Challenged water types call to talk about themselves. Only at the tail end of a conversation may they remember to ask about your life. Challenged water types overreact. It is better to agree with them than try to change their minds, for like water they will prevail until they wear down your resistance or wear out your peace of mind.

For those who are out of touch with feeling, water types are a good antidote. If you are inclined to abandon projects in the middle, water will guide you back on track. When you feel emotionally frustrated, a water type can untangle confusion to help you return to equanimity. Water types tend to be able to discern the intricacies surrounding emotional issues more than other types.

The Essential Nature of Water

Expressed Water/Hidden Fire Type

 It is difficult for water/fire types to articulate what they feel because their emotional life feels out of balance with the way they prefer to interact. When stressed, these types can sound condescending. Don't try to convince them your way is better. Give them time to come to terms with integrating their feelings with actions.

This combination can be surprising, and while they may appear demure they have the capacity to be unreserved. My son, Zachary, had a chemistry teacher who most probably was a water/fire type. Ladylike, quiet, and reserved, she had students who did not take any other sciences vying to take her class, to the administration's constant amazement. In the confines of her classroom, she exposed her inner self, and her otherwise demure demeanor changed into that of a consummate entertainer.

Water/fire types can really be hard to read. Their normally calm, sedate exterior belies an interior passionate emotional range. If you are dating a person who will be prim and proper in public, but a mischiefmaker when home, you are in the company of a water/fire type.

What Expressed Water/Hidden Fire
Types Need in Their Space

When the rift is too deep between the outward expression and the inward feelings, add earth. When water/fire types feel misunder-

stood, adding earth will help them find a way to access and articulate their emotions appropriately. Like a pot resting on burners,
water/fire types are slow to boil, but once they do, nothing short of
removing them from a situation can help. Plush cushions, down
comforters, and all fabrics that feel comfortable to the touch are
good for this type. Since water and fire are both catalysts, water/fires
sometimes feel as if they have no way to manifest themselves.

Calming influence for a water/fire type's emotional life

Greenhouses attached to windows are beneficial and a comforting way to bring in the wood element. Wood elements can give
water/fire types the impetus to express themselves through actions
rather than internalize. For apartment dwellers, lots of plants grouped
together can alleviate the frustration of having too many feelings and
not enough suitable avenues for expression.

Expressed Water/Hidden Earth Type

Farmers call a light drizzle a "lady
rain" because it falls deliberately
and steadily without the drama of
a downpour that grabs the topsoil
and carries it away. A water/earth
combination flourishes with consistency and can be gravely sabo-
taged by lack of harmony. While these types have emotions close
to the surface, they can be relied on and in fact can provide the
kind of consistent emotional support that is excellent at the core of

a relationship. The challenge for them is to nurture themselves, for without any charged, forward impetus in their makeup they tend to try to be accommodating without deep consideration for their own feelings.

Since water completely invades its surroundings, water/earth people are often unable to access their earth emotions, which seek harmony and insist on loyalty. Although they appear to go with the flow, be certain to acknowledge their desires, for although they feel strongly, they typically don't express how strongly.

What Expressed Water/Hidden Earth Types Need in Their Space

The ideal element to introduce into their environment is wood. Onyx-green accessories on low tables or copper with a greenish cast on picture frames, occasional tables, and wind chimes are a few acceptable suggestions. Sofas with classic modern lines and ladderback chairs provide the horizontal wood line that feels right to the water/earth person.

When you add metal, this type's decisive emotional nature gains the upper hand. When there are important decisions to make, a dinner with a table set with white roses, silver bowls, or candlesticks can help this type trust his or her intuition.

Fire elements feel out of sync with water/earth because both of these elements are susceptible to fire's assault. One of my students, a Boston attorney, was stunned when I told her not to wear the red sweater she had on that day in class when with her husband. "How did you know my husband hated this sweater?" she asked, astonished. She had, during her turn at having the class "feng shui" her home, described him enough so that I knew he was likely a water/earth type and would find the color red agitating. Fire's color red would annoy him, especially on weekdays, when he was exhausted from working long hours.

Expressed Water/Hidden Metal Type

When undecided or perplexed, water/metal people will become detached. Just when you think you have stirred them emotionally, they will back off. Water/metal will withdraw when challenged, leaving a situation rather than facing confrontation. Metal needs time to mull things over, carefully considering all aspects, and is at odds with water's effusiveness. Water/metal types may intimate that they have made a decision long before they are actually comfortable with it. Don't expect to influence this type, for they will inevitably follow their heart.

My aunt Bibi's husband became intrigued by her when she was engaged to another man. This did not deter him from pursuing her, and he would intimidate her suitor by waiting on her doorstep when my aunt and her fiancé returned home from a date. No prodding or coaxing persuaded my future uncle to stop, and finally his persistence wore down the fiancé and won my aunt's heart. No doubt my uncle Herbert is a water/metal person.

What Expressed Water/Hidden Metal Types Need in Their Space

If a water/metal person is stuck in a rut, add fire. Bursts of purple, red, and fuchsia can help them overcome resistance to change. This type does well surrounded by bright colors and bold prints. In fact muted, wishy-washy prints can, in the long run, cause them to feel depressed. Introducing a bit more metal into their environment with shiny picture frames, mirrors, and items covered with high-gloss paints prevents their constrained emotional life from being consumed by their propensity to emote.

If you have ever been around a worry wart, you may be looking squarely in the face of a water/metal person. Because they care and because it is hard for them to let go, water/metal types tend to fret. Action distracts them and allays their fears. Wind-up music boxes, mobiles, and ceiling fans are good antidotes for worry.

Once water/metal types find their heart's desire in work and love, they can get down to the business of becoming accomplished. The wood element, as represented by pinstripes on pillowcases and towels, sandblasted striped drinking glasses, and lots of real plants or paintings and fabrics representing vines, trellises, or a verdant wooded scene, can help them feel settled and focused.

When life is unstable because of a loss, move, or job change, add earth. This will solidify a sense of security. Use glazed tiles as hot plates on a dinner table, as coasters for their morning coffee or tea, or as pedestals for soap dishes in the kitchen and bathroom. Brown dish towels, washcloths, and rush welcome mats are also a way of adding earth during a transition period.

Expressed Water/Hidden Water Type

Emoting at the slightest provocation, a water/water type has difficulty controlling intense emotions. Decision making is confusing and painful for these people, for they can understand all sides of an issue. It is difficult to get them to pinpoint or explain exactly how they feel because they are generally overwhelmed by all kinds of feelings. Don't put them on the spot with even simple questions like what movie they want to see or what they want for supper.

However, if you are hurting and want someone who is willing to listen to you and wait for you to explain yourself fully, water/water types are the ones to seek out. Compassion is their calling card, and jobs that require empathy are complementary to their elemental nature.

What Expressed Water/Hidden Water Types Need in Their Space

Having only the water catalyst in one's makeup can stymie actualization. Adding lots of earth, especially across from their bed, desk, and dining room seat, can capture their elusiveness and convert it to resolve. Choose photographs of desert scenes or bare mountains like the red rocks of Sedona, Arizona, to express the earth element suitably. Coarse textures like burlap can check emotions and provide a needed mechanism for expression.

Keep a home warm and dry and try to direct water/water types to engage in activities in sunny rooms. It is best if their daily work room faces the direction of the sun. Nonshiny metal can also shore up their indecisive quality. Wrought-iron candlesticks, decorative stair railings, and plant brackets are a few suggestions.

Expressed Water/Hidden Wood Type

Water/wood types typically frustrate themselves. On one hand they dream of accomplishing great things; on the other they act on them so slowly that often the opportune time has passed. It is often their partner's job to stimulate them to take action. This often includes helping them extract the pearl inside a mound of ideas. Collectors are often elementally either water/wood types or wood/water types because water types have the patience to shop and can't easily part with things, while wood types like the opportunity to expand upon anything.

While wood types tend to like anyone exciting, water types will be more circumspect in deciding whom to let into their lives. Wood people can work even without a clear-cut ending, while water types have the capacity to transcend difficulties, using every available resource to get where they desire. The combination of the two is very powerful. Water/wood people do not typically appear to be so potent, but when they choose to go after a goal they will keep applying themselves until they achieve it.

What Expressed Water/Hidden Wood Types Need in Their Space

Wood/water types often suffer from the cold, but rather than turning up the thermostat for the room, cover them with a thick wool comforter on the sofa and a goose-down duvet on the bed. Water/wood types need tactile comforting.

Water/wood people tend to make plans but don't always carry them out. Want to make this type commit? Add a spark of fire with earth to a scene. Burgundy throw pillows, red clay mugs, or a pale green fern can capture attention and incite them to action.

Capture a water/wood's attention by placing a fire symbol in view.

Full of ideas that are often not actualized, these people live with more regrets over what they did not do than what they did. To help them put their ideas and plans into action, add earth to the environment. Chunky, fat-legged tables and thick, medium-to-dark wood tops will absorb their indecision.

BALANCING THE WATER PERSON

Expressed or hidden water can be balanced by the following alterations to the environment.

Balancing Water by Adding Fire

Water types can't escape from fire, so be careful how and where you add fire colors, shapes, and scents. If your intentions are to energize your water type by symbolically drying out his or her emotional overload, carefully and strategically placed fire symbols can do the trick.

Stay away from fire symbols in the dining or work area. Water types like a calm, unruffled atmosphere in which to ruminate. However, to stimulate sensuality with an overworked, fatigued water type, use red candles and cover a bed with an orange coverlet or sheets.

Balancing Water by Adding Earth

For water types who have flooded their lives with too much activity, add earth's color to window treatments. Earth can stop water from dissipating energy. If an earth person lives in a home with large enough rooms, place the furniture away from the walls. In so doing, the center, which is earth's location, will be stabilized.

Balancing Water by Adding Metal

Metal can contain water and help water types give shape to their thoughts. If a water type needs to be prodded into making a decision, add metal's shiny surfaces, round shapes, or strong materials. Metal and water can be a remarkably effective combination as can the colors white (metal) and black (water).

Balancing Water by Adding Water

Adding more water to an overflowing tub is not advisable. Don't use dark colors, wavy lines, and loose-weave fabrics in water's home decor. Since a water person tends to be too involved in the minutiae of emotions, living with more water can squelch the possibility of change. If it is advisable to make changes, remove as many water elements as possible in an environment.

Balancing Water by Adding Wood

In many ways, wood uses water to transform and blossom. Adding wood elements to the homes of water people can help them transcend their own inertia. Wood elements help a water person get in touch with hidden potentials. Give a water type who needs support a plant stand, large-leafed plants, a forest green ceramic holder for pens and pencils or toothbrushes, or furniture with simple lines.

Best Partners for Water

If you are . . .	Your best partnership combination is . . .
water/fire	metal/earth
water/earth	wood/metal
water/metal	wood/water
water/water	wood/metal or metal/wood, earth/metal
water/wood	metal/water, fire/earth
fire/water	earth/metal
earth/water	wood/wood
metal/water	earth/wood
wood/water	water/wood, water/metal

Challenging Partners for Water

If you are . . .	Your challenging partnership combination is . . .
water/fire	earth/water
water/earth	fire/wood
water/metal	wood/fire
water/water	earth/fire or fire/earth
water/wood	fire/water
fire/water	water/earth
earth/water	water/fire
metal/water	fire/earth
wood/water	earth/earth, earth/fire

PARTNERS FOR WATER

The following measures can help balance water's partnerships.

Fire as Water's Partner

Water types are attracted to fire but are often consumed by it. A water type who has either low physical or mental energy should consider carefully before entering a relationship with a fire type because fire types will force water to be actively engaged in activities—or else. Life will not be uneventful with a fire mate; just be careful not to interfere with his or her intentions too frequently and be prepared to keep yourself in peak condition.

Water types like to watch fire's enthusiasm and are rarely depressed or despondent with them as mates. Since fire can penetrate water's defensive armor, water types are forced to change and grow. Sometimes the adjustment is painful and sometimes stimulating.

Lori and her husband Bill are the quintessential fire/water couple. Bill is contemplative and is prone to dwell on ideas or decisions for an inordinately long time. Finally, after many years of marriage, Lori decided to use her fire to alter Bill's naturally slow pace. She took responsibility for designing his work area and added an Oriental carpet, a visitor's chair with a tiny chevron design, and used lamps with triangular shades on the credenza. The fire element worked wonders for Bill, and his business doubled in one year. She, however, has to subjugate her own momentum to be in accord with his. In their case, it worked wonders for Lori because she learned to focus and stay the course instead of following fire's tendency to gobble up lots of activities without delving deeply into one.

Earth as Water's Partner

Earth types help water types become emotionally balanced. An earth/water couple will typically be homebodies because water will be inclined to defer to earth's desire to stay put. Water types can circumvent earth's demands without causing fragmentation or arguments. This combination will typically have a smooth, even relationship, one that is usually not filled with surprises. It is, however, challenging for this combination to last a long time. After a while the water partner will feel obliterated by the consuming presence of the earth partner.

Metal as Water's Partner

Water people admire metal's inventiveness and courage and respect them although they don't always feel understood by them. Over the long haul, water types help metal ones slow down. If a water/metal relationship survives, it will mature and sweeten with time. While metal is the consummate teacher, water is the consummate listener. Water, not always able to condense ideas or plans into action, can rely on metal for help.

Water as Water's Partner

Mix two waters together and you have the ingredients for a great drama. While they both feel understood, they are not terribly capable of helping each other out of personal dilemmas. Without a good outside support system of friends and family, a partnership with two waters can become burdensome and exhausting. It is best for them to add the element of metal and wood into their homes to keep sexual energy charged.

If one partner is a challenged water and the other not, being together can correct the former in the same way as a polluted river can regain its natural balance by having no additional pollutants as well as having clean water continually percolating into it. In a house such features as a sky-blue welcome mat, a painting with shades of blue, or cobalt candlesticks can be a catalyst for change.

Wood as Water's Partner

Water is the power behind a wood's throne. This is the perfect combination so long as the stronger partner is wood. Water will be empowered vicariously by watching his or her partner thrive. If such a relationship dissolves, the water partner will typically be more devastated and will need time to recuperate. To thwart a wood/water partnership from dissolving, especially when the wood is the stronger of the two, decorate a main gathering space with more water elements than wood and little or no earth elements. Wood types can ride the emotional waves that water types are prone to and will tend to remain by their sides even when the emotional climate is intense.

13

WOOD TYPE

Shape: rectangle—all things grow vertically or horizontally

Color: green—the color of photosynthesis or growth

Texture: grainy—visual representation of cells

Direction: east—represents beginnings, the rising sun

Smell/Taste: minty, resinous—the smell of freshness or newness

Sound: reeds, horns—forcing air out requires renewed breath

Season: spring—the season of rebirth

Positive Characteristics of Wood
adventurous
open-minded
capable of leadership
intelligent
truthful
able to thrive under pressure
willing to risk

Challenging Characteristics of Wood
demanding
faultfinding
arrogant

judgmental
opportunistic
impatient

Partner Who Controls Wood

metal

Partner Who Balances Wood

water

Partner Who Supports Wood

earth

Partner Who Is Supported by Wood

earth, fire

Partner Who Is Restrained by Wood

fire, metal

Overview

Wood types are ideal as pioneers, stockbrokers, and inventors. They are likely to sign up for classes and fill seminars on just about any subject. Wood types are not afraid to take risks. They convert ideas to actions and are effective leaders and partners because they either get things done or find someone to do them.

If you want to take a trip around the world, a wood type will be a reasonable, organized, and adventurous traveling companion. While you won't necessarily be skydiving over the Himalayas, you will learn all about the culture, people, and sights of an area. Wood types like to learn and will find opportunities to do so wherever they can.

Wood people excel as leaders because they can expand under pressure yet bend or compromise when necessary just as trees bend to reach the light when blocked by other vegetation. The downside of a wood partner is that if you can't keep up, you might find yourself one of his or her discarded possessions. It is imperative to live actively and at least appreciate change if your partner is a wood person.

Characteristic Choices of Wood Types

If you have ever been in a home with green striped fabrics or wall coverings, plank flooring, and lots of plants, pets, or artifacts, you were most likely in a wood person's home. Wood types gravitate to vertical lines. Tall plants or vines trained to grow up the walls, pedestals, leggy furniture, and four-poster beds are choices wood persons are inclined to make.

Rubber is a favored material of wood, and you may find it in the most unlikely places. I was visiting a gift shop at an art center with a girlfriend when suddenly the silence was penetrated by a shriek. I looked up to see my wood element pal with a rubberized necklace dangling from her hand.

"I just love it," she panted, barely containing her excitement at finding such a treasure. Needless to say, she purchased it, and today it hangs jauntily from a hook on the wall of her bedroom. Male woods might have a penchant for gooseneck lights, chain-link fencing, pull-chain lighting, and foam rubber beer glass coolers. Don't change them; wood types treasure flexible materials.

Green, the color of wood, can be represented in plants and in an overall color scheme. Wood types love the oxidized metal called *verdigris*. Don't confuse the presence of actual wood with the wood element, for most often wood is an earth color. Although striped woods like zebra wood or ones with pronounced vertical grains might represent a wood element, wood types don't have any more interest in actual wood than do other types.

THE ESSENTIAL NATURE OF WOOD

Expressed Wood/Hidden Fire Type

Where there's smoke, there's fire, and wood/fire types are always smoking. While they love to take courses and learn new skills, they absorb information too quickly and can become disruptive to others who need more time. While these people are likely to inject enthusiasm into a project, event, or person, their staying power is marginal. If you are new in town, look for wood/fire people with whom to align yourself; they are likely to be friendly and open and love to make new friends. To keep them interested, take them to interesting, unusual events. Wood types love cigar bars, foreign films, windsurfing, and other hot new activities.

Play hard to get with a wood/fire type. When something is just out of reach, a wood/fire will almost always obsess over how to get it. After finishing one activity, wood/fires are burning to start the next.

What Expressed Wood/Hidden Fire
Types Need in Their Space

Add water to calm wood/fire types down and help them stay focused. To capture their attention or keep them home more often, consider having either a water feature, heavy curtains in classic brocade, or a library of dark wood paneling. Wood/fire types need environments decorated with water/earth elements. Don't be subtle. Use obvious deep blue or fabrics with curved lines. Large urns with tall plants, black leather couches, terra-cotta tile floors, bathrooms with black toilets, sinks, and tubs, and navy blue ceilings or medium-toned wood-paneled rooms are choices that broadly express water or earth.

The younger the person with this elemental combination, the more the earth element is needed. Wood/fire types given to self-doubt or insecurity are helped by small, chunky furniture. Pedestal table bases in tan, brown, or terra-cotta materials, plush stuffed sofa pillows, and trunks for cocktails or end tables are some earth pieces to consider adding when trying to seduce wood/fire types.

Expressed Wood/Hidden Earth Type

Wood/earth types are likely to have no regrets because their personality is in complete control over the emotional aspect of life. Likely to springboard to success, they have the energy to circumvent adversity by changing and learning by their mistakes. If you are lucky enough to live with a wood/earth person, count your blessings. If you are pursuing a wood/earth, be patient and you will be rewarded, because wood/earth is one of the easiest types to live with.

While wood desires to change things, earth has the ability to figure out how to get it done and keep wood controlled—a dynamic combination. If a wood/earth is in your corner, be assured that nothing will stop him or her from finding a way to support you.

What Expressed Wood/Hidden Earth
Types Need in Their Space

Wood/earth types are not likely to stray unless swept away by tides of emotions; therefore, keep the water element to a minimum in this environment. To introduce just a bit of water, hang a picture with a large expanse of sky, use blue placemats or a blue tablecloth or perhaps position a cobalt-blue pen and pencil holder on a desk. The secret element for this type is metal. It is the spark that motivates them to propagate ideas, alter or mend relationships, and accept change. Use shiny surfaces rather than the shape of a circle to introduce metal into an environment. Silver or chrome is better than gold or brass because the color silver is closer to water. In fact, wood/earth types living with a great deal of gold or yellow colors tend to become lethargic and unmotivated.

Expressed Wood/Hidden Metal Type

 Although not likely to be the center of attention, wood/metal types can seduce you with a poetry of words. Often possessing a disarming sense of humor, they can be surprisingly charming. Great to have on a team, be it sports, business, or neighborhood associations. Like bonsai trees, wood/metal will not buckle under pressure and have the ability to survive.

Want to charm a wood/metal type? Discuss obscure topics. These types love to look through your old picture albums and delight in seeing the photographs of a recent trip. While craving emotional rewards, they will not verbalize their needs. For example, a wood person who wants to hold your hand at the movies might not reach for it but rather will wait until you make the first move. Grab a wood/metal type and give him or her a hug when visiting—you will delight him or her immensely!

What Expressed Wood/Hidden Metal Types Need in Their Space

Wood/metal tends to get lost in information and be disconnected from feelings. Adding earth to a wood/metal's environment can dramatically intensify his or her emotional reactions. Large areas like walls, carpets, and window treatments are perfect foils to introduce earth's expressions. Choose chocolate carpeting, tan curtains, coffee-colored walls, musk aromatics, and peaceful ethereal music to compel wood/metal types to confess how they feel.

Like a magnet, this type holds on to ideas and opinions and needs to convince others of their validity. Don't try to separate wood/metal types from what they are doing unless you have a great deal of the water element in an environment. Fluorescent full-spectrum light and pale blue will help them be more flexible and less intense.

Expressed Wood/Hidden Water Type

Wood/water types always seem to be on top of things yet constantly get pulled under by unforeseen circumstances. Don't cry on the shoulder of a wood/water type you are trying to attract, for these people spend far too much time dwelling on their own emotional life to have much energy for others. I recently hired a wood/water type to build an Internet page. While I was dazzled by the presentation, the drama of getting him to complete it wiped me out. Although wood types tend to be excellent communicators, when their emotional element is water they tend to emote and use words to diffuse their feeling of being overwhelmed and overburdened. Arguing with them won't help; let them finish and then state your case. They will, of course, always have a retort.

On the upside, wood/water types have the capacity to nurture themselves. If you are involved in a career or your children, having a wood/water type as a partner will eliminate the need for you to make excuses when wanting to work over the weekend or not having dinner prepared.

What Expressed Wood/Hidden Water
Types Need in Their Space

Fire and earth are the elements that, in the right proportions, can produce a balance for a wood/water type. Since their creativity needs sharpening and unclogging, fire can nudge them to move forward. Quilts with red or triangular patterns, red clay objects, red beads, or rose quartz geodes can support them to clarify their priorities.

To win their hearts, be supportive when they are emotionally needy. Give them a shoulder to cry on and a basket of pears or bananas. Light-colored earth elements are ideal to help them contain their emotions and get on with the business of living. Tans, beiges, sands, and yellows can be incorporated with red in fabrics, rugs, wall coverings, and bedsheets. Gold-trimmed flatware, dishes,

and glasses help them feel settled daily. Antique brass or bronze art-
fully placed can help them put words into action.

Expressed Wood/Hidden Wood Type

 Inventive, unafraid, and the first to
learn about or buy the newest gad-
get or agree with an innovative idea,
wood/wood types typically move at
the speed of lightning. They have a
penchant for self-destruction because they are too interested in
change and may burn their bridges. Boredom is the most lethal card
you can deal them. Don't expect them to be content to take a cruise
around the world. They are likely to rush into action, and even
when inappropriate, they seem to be in a hurry. Good teachers of
gifted classes, wood/wood types are intent about learning. They tend
to believe the grass is greener elsewhere, so it is up to you to fill
their lives with surprises. Whisk them away on vacations, try new
restaurants, take them to lectures, and fill their time with unique
events and situations.

Wood/wood types tend to get worked up about things even
when they have not yet happened. My father used to tell this joke
to illustrate why one should not make a mountain out of a mole-
hill as some wood/wood types tend to do:

A car broke down when a family was enjoying a Sunday drive
in the country. The husband volunteered to walk the three or four
miles back to where a gas station had been sighted. During the first
mile he worried that the gas station would be closed. If it was,
would he be able to find the owner's home? Since this was a small
town, he rationalized, neighbors were likely to know where the gas
station owner lived.

Somewhere along miles two and three he imagined he found
the owner of the gas station at home eating Sunday dinner with his
family. In his mind, he pleaded with the owner to take time out and
fill a gas can for him to carry back to his stranded car. The man
became infuriated when the owner announced he didn't want to be
disturbed on his one day off.

By this time the man had reached the real gas station and was
so infuriated by his mental scenario that when he saw the atten-
dant, he blurted out, "Hey, you, take your gas and shove it!"

Wood/wood types have vivid imaginations and can jump to
perplexing conclusions.

What Expressed Wood/Hidden Wood Types Need in Their Space

Since wood/wood types desire action for action's sake, metal can help consolidate their ideas so the actions can take form. Glass-topped tables supported by metal bases, large metal hardware on cabinets, and wall-mounted metal lights can be an ideal way to introduce metal. Just as a fence can restrain a pet from injuring itself, metal can inhibit wood/wood's natural inclination to go too far out on a limb. If you are living with a wood/wood type, be prepared to stay busy thwarting him or her from taking foolhardy risks.

When there is little to interfere with its growth, a tree will grow straight and tall. In the same way, wood/wood types who have been single for a long time can be unyielding and require some gentle prodding to make them pliable. Stringed instruments, such as harp, piano, or xylophone, can help wood/wood types get in touch with the feelings of those around them.

BALANCING THE WOOD PERSON

Expressed or hidden wood can be balanced by the following alterations to the environment.

BALANCING WOOD BY ADDING FIRE

A drop of fire can spark wood types to stop what they are doing and consider the consequences. The fire element can force woods to focus in on the here and now. For example, sports enthusiasts who spend most of their free time watching televised sporting events might need fire to help them pause to ponder the situation long enough to see if they need to alter their behavior. However, most woods do not do well with a great deal of fire elements surrounding them. Fire chips away at wood's integrity or destroys its natural state. Reds, intense prints, rough surfaces, and too much time spent facing a southern exposure can sap wood of its vitality.

BALANCING WOOD BY ADDING EARTH

Earth supports wood types. The colors of earth, brown, terra-cotta, or pale sand tones help wood types on their chosen path. Just like a rich, thick layer of earth can supply actual wood with nutrients to grow to capacity, an earth environment can provide wood persons with the support to take risks they normally wouldn't. Wood people who are athletes can be enervated by too much earth in a home. Dark ceilings or floor-to-ceiling paneling can drain a wood type. However, placing earth in the lower half of a room can brace wood and help him or her feel secure. However, be cognizant of the fact that too many earth elements can stifle enthusiasm for investigation, just as stuffing oneself at the dinner table can kill enthusiasm for accomplishing anything productive afterward.

BALANCING WOOD BY ADDING METAL

While metal is part of the nutrients that wood absorbs from the soil, when it is extracted it becomes a material that can conquer wood. In most cases metal is denser, stronger, and harder than wood. Adding shiny, metallic surfaces or repeated circles in patterns to a wood's environment can cause confusion, frustration, and seriously undermine wood's momentum. Metal is a reflective surface, and wood types tend to act rather than reflect, so wood people feel out of sync with too much metal around them.

BALANCING WOOD BY ADDING WATER

A little water feeds the best of wood's characteristics; too much water overwhelms. However, a bedroom is a perfect place to introduce water. Wood types often need the calming effect of water to be encouraged to touch base with their emotions. Without some water in an environment, wood types are likely to be too pedantic and self-righteous. If you want a wood type to be receptive to an idea or a request, give a gift that contains water colors and shapes. Wood types feel more amenable to suggestions when quieted by the effects of water.

In an office or a home's main gathering space, too much water can overpower a healthy wood's natural enthusiasm. However, challenged wood types might benefit from having their tendencies subdued. Use water elemental colors and shapes to control a challenged wood.

BALANCING WOOD BY ADDING WOOD

A tree in a forest grows slower than a solitary one in a field. Adding wood to a wood type's environment can slow the person down and temper enthusiasm for change. Wood types need good lighting

(fire) and water to develop to their full potential. Don't use greenery or too many tall, slim candles on a table when entertaining a
wood person. Floating candles with vines trailing across the table
or down the side of a vase will expand the wood person's capacity for relaxation.

Best Partners for Wood

If you are . . .	Your best partnership combination is . . .
wood/fire	earth/wood, water/earth
wood/earth	earth/metal
wood/metal	earth/water
wood/water	water/metal
wood/wood	water/earth or earth/water, earth/metal
fire/wood	earth/water
earth/wood	metal/water
metal/wood	earth/water
water/wood	wood/earth

Challenging Partners for Wood

If you are . . .	Your challenging partnership combination is . . .
wood/fire	metal/water
wood/earth	fire/wood
wood/metal	metal/metal
wood/water	fire/fire, water/water
wood/wood	fire/metal or metal/fire, wood/fire
fire/wood	water/water
metal/wood	earth/fire
earth/wood	fire/metal
water/wood	earth/metal

PARTNERS FOR WOOD

The following measures can help balance wood's partnerships.

Fire as Wood's Partner

Wood types can be inspired by fire only if both partners are equally
successful and mature. While they both are naturally adventurous
and ready to experience new ideas and situations, a fire partner will

typically outshine wood in social situations, which can cause the wood to feel jealous and competitive.

Earth as Wood's Partner

When a wood person needs a solid foundation from which to spring, choose an earth partner. Earth types can be inspirational to wood, for they will contribute the perspiration for wood's inspirations. Artist, writer, and musician wood types should seek earth partners, for they typically will keep a home running smoothly. Earth partners can be the single most important impetus to a wood's success, especially when wood types need time to uncover their special niche in life. Traditionally, it is better for the male to be wood and the female earth.

Earth types value loyalty, while wood seeks to succeed, sometimes at the expense of tradition. So while this partnership is good for a wood partner, it is more challenging for one with earth.

Metal as Wood's Partner

Wood and metal may be a tricky combination, for metal types talk about ideas and wood types take action. A metal person can be resistant to wood's enthusiastic approach to change. Don't let your ardor be dampened, because metals typically will come around; it's just that they need to feel it's their idea. This partnership has great potential to be intensely interesting because both will be on a quest to develop and learn. Sometimes, if the fields are too diverse, their paths may separate.

Water as Wood's Partner

Wood types need water to thrive. Wood types' ardor for whatever they are interested in can affect their focus on an emotional life. Having a water person around will help them stay connected to feelings, not just ideas. So primal is their interconnection that wood/water partners are likely to have a rich, rewarding physical intimacy.

Wood as Wood's Partner

Wood/wood is the stuff of pioneer teams. Not likely to be fearful, wood partners happily explore outer or inner space together. As a couple they enjoy making friends and can assimilate and adjust to new situations and places. While they are mutually supportive, they don't have the constitution to be drained by the other's needs. When both partners are strong, wood couples are amazing and fun to watch in action.

The only fly in the ointment for this partnership is if they have very different philosophies and belief systems. Be aware that woods are not likely to change fundamentally or philosophically, so don't go into a relationship thinking you can change this partner.

Part III

SCOPE-ING ROOMS

How a room is used reveals a great deal about an individual. For the most part, rooms are assigned specific functions. We gather in a living or family room, eat in a dining room, sleep in a bedroom, and cook in a kitchen. The degree to which we vary from normal use and the subtleties within each room describe how we feel about the activity normally pursued in that room. Our priorities, how we relate to people, our ideas, and what activities we are comfortable exposing are unveiled for the discerning person to see. This section is devoted to a room-by-room analysis and describes some common signs that tip off an observer to feelings, motivations, and elemental proclivities.

> **How a room is used can reveal how one relates to people, ideas, and activities.**

The first step in any analysis is to look for red flags. Red flags are signs that something may be amiss or a problem. There usually are observable signs in an environment warning us of some characteristic or proclivity that might be problematic in a lover if we were to enter into long-term intimacy with him or her. Red flags can be obvious, like the woman who sleeps on her sofa and uses her bedroom for her hobbies, or they can be more elusive, such as a kitchen that is just a little too dark or a gathering room with the only comfortable seating facing a television. Some obvious red flags are:

locked closets
every closet and cabinet filled to capacity
unusual clutter
unusual emptiness
frayed, worn-out, marred, or otherwise visibly imperfect
    furniture
visible dirt or grime
too little light
too much light
no conversational seating
no dining facility
broken doorbell
unmade bed
overflowing garbage
no cocktail table in front of a sofa
no food in a refrigerator
no personalization or accessory at an entrance door

If you observe one red flag, don't be too put off. This person may need support in one particular area. However, if there are multiple red flags, be cautious. You may have more potentially toxic issues than you care to deal with.

The next step is to identify dominant elements in the environment to begin to determine the resident's personal elements and whether or not this person would be a good match for your elemental nature. More often than not, we furnish our home with the elements that best express us. Public rooms typically display the elements that characterize a person's personality, and private space—bedrooms, bathrooms, and sometimes hobby rooms and offices—tend to express the emotional or hidden elements.

> **Public rooms typically contain the elements that express one's personality and private rooms the elements representing emotions.**

For example, a wood/fire person could have a tailored sofa and chair, lots of plants, and striped curtains in the gathering room and a burgundy bedspread, nubby carpet, and copper-framed wall art in the bedroom. Since the wood element is expressed in rectangular lines and the color green and fire is expressed in colors near red and rough surfaces, you could deduce correctly that this person's expressed element was wood and his or her hidden element was fire.

Claire Cooper Marcus's book, *House as a Mirror of Self*, suggests that choices made for a home can relate expressly to childhood events, beliefs, and images. Marcus's book or a psychologist can help you learn more about yourself or someone else by understanding the formative influences of the past. This book is limited to looking at how certain preferences in objects generally indicate certain personality traits and emotional inclinations. For our purposes the choice of an expensive leather recliner is significant in that its brown color and chunky shape suggest the element earth and all of earth's associated characteristics. Why the chair's owner has placed it squarely in front of a large TV and why he or she watches a lot of TV is not addressed here. Combining the two types of knowledge will, however, broaden your insight into this person and how compatible a partner he or she might be for you. As you read about scope-ing in Part III of this book, remember that everything you learn about a person through feng shui must be interpreted in the full context of the person's life, past, present, and even future.

Whatever you discover through scope-ing should be viewed only as one more layer of information about someone, not as an absolute edict to pursue or reject the person. Only you know if you can live with someone whose home has a constant stream of visitors or if you will be annoyed by aligning yourself with someone who has not found a way to express his or her creativity. The more you know, however, the better able you are to choose someone who will ultimately be a good love match.

14

THE ENTRANCES, EXTERIOR AND INTERIOR

T he word *relationships* begins with *relate*. The first visible sign of who we are and how we relate is generated at a threshold. The attention paid to a threshold expresses the care we are likely to extend to others.

Most of us can remember our first day of school or the first day at a job. First impressions leave an indelible mark on our psyche that influences the future. I remember my first day at junior high school. Wearing an outfit that had been selected with great care to help me appear sophisticated, I dashed from the car, waved my mother off quickly, and melted into a crowd waiting for the morning bell to summon us inside. Suddenly, a friend from elementary school pulled at my sleeve and dragged me in the direction of the girl with the bright pink lips.

"She's in our class," my friend confided in a stage whisper.
Stunned, I was flabbergasted that someone our age would
wear lipstick.
"What color do you think that is?" I asked, trying not to
seem too impressed.
"Let's ask!" was my friend's reply.

So on that bright but cloud-dappled fall day, I summoned the courage to ask her for the name of the lipstick. "Sweetheart pink" is etched in my memory forever, while decades later images of classes, teachers, and schoolmates have blended into the amorphous soup of memories.

Imagine visiting your home for the first time. How does the initial experience represent you? Does it communicate what you want?

It may be startling to think about what the entrance communicates to a person who has never visited before. Although you may lack conscious awareness of all that is within your field of vision when entering a house, know that your first response to a home is via an entrance's visual impressions. What is the message that greets you each time you return home?

Exterior Entrances

Positive Signs at the Exterior Entrance of a Home

cared-for landscape
healthy vegetation
flowers
shoveled or cleared walkways
well-maintained exterior
clearly identified entrance door
place to sit
personal objects such as a gazing ball, wind chime, ceramics, etc.
visible and tended doorbell, knocker, or other way to summon those inside

Red Flags at an Exterior Entrance of a Home (may indicate problems with self-esteem or relating appropriately to others)

overgrown vegetation
dull landscaping
diseased trees
cracked sidewalk
broken steps
damaged screen doors
out-of-order doorbells
no obvious way to summon those inside (no doorbell, door knocker, etc., in sight)
no personal accessories

Common Symbols Displayed in Outside Entrances That Express Particular Elements

In addition to observing the color, line, and shape of objects used in this area, the following symbols can reinforce a person's elemental type. Entrances are like personalities, for they are the exteriors that interact with others.

Fire

pine trees (planted by the occupant)
pole light
picket fence
slanted-roof birdhouses
peaked-roof mailboxes
red flags, wind socks, or gazing balls

Earth

low ground cover
trimmed, neat bushes
deer licks
rocks
yellow flags, wind socks, or gazing balls

Metal

sundials
globe pole lights
topiary balls
tire swing
tube mailboxes
white, gold, or silver flags, wind socks, or
    gazing balls

Water

water feature such as birdbaths, fountains,
    waterfalls, etc.
curved flower beds
black stepping-stones
garden umbrellas
overhead ceiling of vegetation
chain fencing
blue or black flags, wind socks, or gazing balls

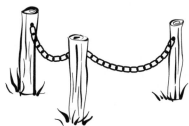

*Draped chains or rope fences are a
water element.*

Wood

straight pathways
swings
picket fences
flags
trellis covered sparsely with vines
wind socks with green or stripes

An approach to a home expresses the face you hope to show others. How much care has been given to the pathway leading to the door? Is all well tended or in disrepair? Not caring for an entrance often mirrors not caring for one's appearance, and focusing too much on an entrance often portends of paying too much attention.

Sociability can also be predicted from the exterior entrance. The house of one of my neighbors has no visible pathway, artwork, nameplates, garden decor, or even the street's number at the entrance. Needless to say, I am not surprised when they never show up at neighborhood parties and gatherings. An exterior entrance extends the border of home. It is proclaiming self-esteem and involvement with and toward others. What you see when approaching a home foreordains not only how you will be treated but indicates the depth of another's ability to relate or empathize with others.

The difference between a person who hangs a decorative flag outside the home and one who mounts a special door knocker or bell is that the first wants to be noticed and the second wants you to feel comfortable when visiting. A flag can be seen at a greater distance and calls attention to the house no matter who is traveling down a street. A bell is more intimate, because you have to be close to the entrance to see it. A bell usually is the first direct contact a guest has with a home, and its location, appearance, and sound reveal whether the owner pays attention to other people's needs. After all, a home owner rarely rings his or her own doorbell.

Which Door Do You Enter?

No one would invite the president of the United States into a home through the side door. Which door you are ushered through will depend on the impression the owner wishes to make and how highly valued your presence is. If you are ushered through a side door, you will more likely be greeted by demands in the future. Moreover, those who use a utility entrance or ask their guest to do so are likely to spend more time working than relaxing.

Even though the square footage of a contemporary house is larger today than it has been in the past, much socializing takes place away from home. Further, with the continued movement to even more dispersed suburbs, commuting time has increased the workday to ten, twelve, and sometimes fourteen hours. Many discover that they have more space but less time to enjoy it. To refrain from home being just a place to store one's stuff and sleep, one should focus on making an entrance to a home even more significant. If someone enters home through a nonservice door, they are likely conferring significance to home as a haven. If they enter home by way of a pantry, kitchen, or laundry room, perhaps they are emphasizing the responsibilities of guardianship. It is for you to decide if you want to be with someone who is more involved with feelings of home as refuge or someone who believes home is just a stopping-off place between appointments. Be alert to why a utility entrance is used instead of a main one.

INTERIOR ENTRANCES

The first view inside a home can either be life affirming or crippling to positive resolve. Imagine entering a foyer featuring a dazzling flower arrangement perched on an elegant shelf, with comfortable lighting illuminating a soothing painting and a comfortably thick carpet underfoot. These symbols and comforts bespeak the owner's caring and self-esteem.

Flowers indicate mindfulness. Taking the time to purchase and display fresh flowers demands a focus on the here and now. Where there are fresh flowers, there is a person who cares about details. Using candles can also connote attention to detail, as well as a desire to help those who enter feel at ease. When I entered my friend Tacy's home after a cross-country flight, I was greeted by an ethereal glow as the sun dipped below the horizon. Although she had recently been widowed, Tacy had gone out of her way to make my arrival welcoming by lighting all the candles in her house.

Entrances are normally small, compact spaces and can be separate rooms or partitioned areas of a larger room. Even when not large enough to contain furnishings, an entrance can have a dramatic touch of color, handsome accessories mounted on a small shelf, or a patterned area rug. In other words, there is no excuse for leaving a space completely empty and not offering a sign of welcome.

Positive Signs in an Interior Entrance

tidy
doorknobs that function adequately
flowers or plants
candles or special lights
partially empty closet
seasonal adornments
chair
love seat
screen
bench
secretary
grandfather clock
repository for umbrellas or walking sticks
table large enough for packages or a handbag

Red Flags in an Interior Entrance (may indicate a lack of focus on the needs of oneself and others)

broken light switch
insufficient light
closet in which there is no room for a guest's coat
no table or credenza
coats thrown over a chair
shoes haphazardly stationed
no floor mat
breakable artwork or curios

Common Symbols Displayed in Inside Entrances That Express Particular Elements

In addition to the color, line, and shape of objects used in this area, the following symbols can reinforce the person's elemental type. Since foyers are public rooms, the elements expressed there are more often than not a person's expressed self. One's personality is often revealed succinctly in an interior entrance space.

Fire

red or orange fabric, paint, flowers, wall
  covering, accessories, doormat, or carpeting
chevron or triangular prints or patterns on
  accessories

conical lamp shades
sconces
bells
plants with pointed leaves
geometric-style paintings

Earth

tan, brown, or deep yellow fabric, paint,
    flowers, wall covering, accessories,
    doormat, or carpeting
square, squat, or legless furniture
square umbrella holders
geodes
pottery
chair rail dividing the wall into smaller sections
tile flooring or mirrors
landscape paintings

Metal

white, gold, silver, or copper fabric, paint,
    flowers, wall covering, accessories,
    doormat, or carpeting
oval or round vases, doormats, globes for lamps
dream catchers
shields
mirror
gold-leaf frames
paintings with snow, sunsets, or many clouds

Water

blue or black fabric, paint, flowers, wall
    covering, accessories, doormat, or carpeting
any staggered or dissimilar groupings such as
    several standing framed photographs
mobiles
soft music
thick, decorative rope
bell pulls
hanging baskets with cascading vines
paintings with water or nighttime scapes

Wood

 green fabric, paint, flowers, wall covering,
    accessories, doormat, or carpeting
stripes and vertical patterns
umbrellas or walking sticks
decorative beams
columns
tall planters
paintings of trees, jungle scenes, or buildings
    with columns or vertical siding

Ask yourself what makes you feel welcome when you enter a home. If the answer is "nothing," take note. It is not possible to cherish, support, and encourage oneself or another human being without attending to what is experienced first. If there are items indicating an element that is not in accord with yours, be prepared to confront issues that this element triggers. An entrance is a home's first greeting. Is its message positive?

15

GATHERING
ROOMS

We expose our deeply held beliefs about socialization in rooms designed for gathering. The formality or casualness of the room called *living room, den, family room,* or *great room* represents the character of interchange we desire to have. Gathering spaces are enclaves of community, microcosms of how we feel about connecting with others.

Style does not necessarily determine how relaxed a setting feels. Formal gathering spaces can be comfortable, and so-called family settings can inhibit feeling at ease. Are the fabrics easily soiled or damaged? Is the seating set up for large groups? Are there breakable artifacts in easily accessible areas? Are surfaces of tables easily marred? When an area has to be patrolled for violators or requires vigilant observation, the hosts are kept from entertaining effortlessly. If you find a coaster slipped under every drink served, perhaps the surfaces are too fragile and the person too concerned with appearances rather than communication.

How comfortable and accessible the seating is, how flattering and appropriate the lighting is, and how many precariously positioned objects are near pathways or seating are evidence of how much time the host spends there as well as how strongly he or she cares about making others feel at ease. A gathering room so cluttered with objects that seating or a positive ambience is compromised indicates the desire to be left alone. The more roadblocks to comfort, the more roadblocks to intimacy.

**A gathering room cluttered with
objects blocks intimacy.**

A childhood friend's home had sofas lined up against one wall in a gathering room. Fourteen running feet of seating gave little access to agreeable interaction. Feeling like ducks in a row, people who sat on the sofas found communication almost impossible. This family rarely ate dinner or vacationed together.

If furniture is not set up to make interaction easy, you can assume those who live there don't care to socialize and/or communicate. However, living rooms are a case where you should determine a person's history before judging him or her on the basis of the decor. I grew up in a home where the children were not permitted use of the living room. Reserved for company, the living room of the middle class in the 1950s emulated the lifestyles of the socially elite, as did Mother and her friends. To them formal spaces equaled success.

My friend Sara grew up poor in Mississippi. Her mother worked as a domestic and often took Sara along. She remembers the houses her mother worked in as nothing less than castles. Today her home's decor is reminiscent of what was popular for southern upper-middle-class families during that era. Expensive Chinese porcelain lamps flank a curved-back Victorian sofa, and crystal candlesticks sit atop a carved ebony chest/cocktail table in her gathering room. Ali Baba footstools with rakish tassels hanging from a tufted cushion sidle up to a coffee table, creating a dramatic foil for the painted Chinese ebony screens. Sara would love to be seen in the same way as she viewed her mother's employers, and her gathering room stretches to make that statement. What's interesting to note is that the gathering space off the kitchen, which is used by her husband and her, is casual, comfortable, and modern. Which room projects the real Sara? Seek to understand why one would have two distinctly different gathering spaces.

Edward T. Hall, in his book *Hidden Dimension*, observed the flow of conversation between people and discovered that when two people are positioned across from each other they have less interaction than when seated diagonally.

*People converse more when seated across a
diagonal than directly across from each other.*

Our biological heritage prepares us to take action when face-
to-face. When a person is positioned directly across from you, your
vital organs are more vulnerable. In prehistoric times human survival depended on being savvy when facing an animal or a stranger.
Although today we do not usually worry about someone harming
us, what was once an effective evolutionary strategy takes thousands
upon thousands of years to alter. We are naturally prepared for flight
or fight when one on one; therefore sofas or chairs located across
from each other will not promote the same intimate connections as
ones positioned at right angles. This information is known on a deep
intuitive level, and the choice of how seating is arranged can
uncover an attitude about sociability and communication.

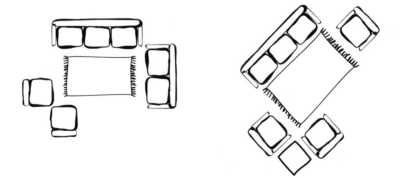

Seating on three sides encourages conversation.

Having three sides to a conversational group is a sign that communication is encouraged. Today we are more likely to see chairs or sofas positioned on only two sides because watching television frequently seems to be more important than conversation. Television has taken the place of the hearth, and families gather around its glow as if it were life supporting. No wonder conversation is a lost art. Those who orient a major portion of the seating in a gathering space toward a television relinquish the rewards of human connections. When television is the focus of a room and positioned on the power wall, you will be choosing someone who may value being entertained more than companionship.

In addition to positioning, note the number of creature comforts placed in the main gathering space. Afghans tossed over arms of a sofa, soft throw pillows to be used under one's head, coffee table books providing diversion, and savory treats within arm's reach are signs of welcome.

> **The seeds of intimacy are planted in compassion, and compassion is expressed by providing comforts.**

While we rarely think of flooring as anything more than a decorative accent, the comfort it provides should be noted when scope-ing a main gathering space. A carpeted floor is often used for extra seating. When area rugs over wood or tile floors do not extend beyond a furniture's boundary, no provision is being made for casual seating.

Finally, observe what objects express personal history and values and if there is a common theme. Noting these and what they suggest can be revealing. Those who are less inclined to be with people often prefer art with inanimate objects, such as still lifes, buildings, street scenes, or abstractions. On the other hand, an obsession with only men, women, or children can be equally telling. The walls of the self-centered female ballroom dancer filled with paintings or photographs of herself telegraph a clear message of self-importance. Another home filled with hunting paraphernalia and photographs of lions overwhelming prey succinctly communicates a macho vitality. If you don't feel comfortable with the subject matter of art, you probably won't feel comfortable in a relationship with the person who chose it.

Collecting can be a positive, relaxing pastime or a challenging, consuming force. On a trip to Key West, I befriended Mary, who dragged me into every store that hinted at the possibility of having replicas of frogs. Unbeknownst to me, Mary's vacations were devoted to enlarging her gargantuan collection of frogs. Her obsessiveness obscured human interaction by its narrow focus. Collectors can be insufferably boring to be with because they demand exclusive attention to their needs. Only if you both are consumed with the same enthusiasm is it fun to be with an overtly passionate collector.

Subject matter is significant. Collections of cow memorabilia, for example, indulge our sense of humor, whereas a collection of, say, helmets would not. Are the collected objects representative of power, humor, or humanity? Do they connect to the past or present? A writer who collects antique typewriters or quill pens is most likely displaying a love of his or her field and a connection to its history. A writer who collects modern reference books, on the other hand, is likely to be more focused on the here and now.

My friend Michael collects matchbooks on his business travels around the world. Although he might puff on a cigar once in a while, he finds matchbooks decorative and a diversion on his frequent business trips. In Michael's case, collecting is a positive distraction. While collecting frogs gives Mary something to do with her life, collecting matchbooks is for Michael merely a pleasant diversion during otherwise lonely times.

In the best sense a place to gather should be inviting, comfortable, and filled with enough personal items to give the room a distinctive flair. Comfortable, climate friendly, and filled with options, a gathering space should be a place to read, socialize, play games, listen to music, communicate, watch videos or television, and hang out. A gathering space reveals how we feel about community, friendships, and our responsibility to others.

Collections reveal what is revered or can be a leisure time diversion.

Positive Signs in a Gathering Space

U-shaped seating groups
creature comforts dispersed throughout

general and specific illumination
tables within reach of seating
sofa and chairs with arms
some floor covering over tile or wood
diversity of art forms
snacks
games
well-tended plants
trays perched on tables
books, magazines, or newspapers
family photographs

Red Flags in a Gathering Space (*may indicate a lack of commitment to connecting with others*)

furniture positioned to face a TV
armless chairs or sofas
tightly upholstered or hard seating
few personal mementos
too much art devoted to one theme
inadequate lighting, too dark or too bright
nothing alive—plants, animals, etc.
nothing to snack on

COMMON SYMBOLS DISPLAYED IN GATHERING ROOMS THAT EXPRESS PARTICULAR ELEMENTS

In addition to color, line, and shape of objects, the following symbols can reinforce a person's elemental type. Since gathering spaces are public rooms, they reveal more qualities of a person's public or expressed persona than his or her emotional life.

Fire

red or orange fabric, paint, flowers, wall
    covering, accessories, doormat,
    or carpet
flame-stitch- or chevron-patterned upholstery,
    window treatments, or carpeting
Oriental rugs
triangular lamp shades
pyramidal or conical accessories
candles

collections of bows, guns, swords, and animal
skins

art with themes of war, violence, volcanoes, pine
trees, flames, wings, and turrets

Earth

terra-cotta, deep yellow, or brown fabric, paint,
flowers, wall covering, accessories, doormat,
or carpet

square-patterned or checkered upholstery,
window treatments, or carpeting

ceramic containers

club chairs

wooden or square coffee tables

thick legs on furniture

love seats or two-seat sofas

geodes or rocks

dark wood furniture (unpainted)

collections of pottery, geodes, boxes, dark wood
artifacts, chessboards, farm tools, and stamps

art with themes of deserts, mother and child,
close-up of mountains, farms, pueblos,
picnics, and pottery

Metal

white, silver, gold, or copper fabric, paint,
flowers, wall covering, accessories, doormat,
or carpet

dots or circular-patterned upholstery,
window treatments, or carpeting

brass, silver, or copper lamps

round cocktail tables

metallic accessories

mirrors

metal trim

metallic hardware such as door pulls, brackets,
light switches, etc.

collections of round paperweights, coins, jewelry,
watches, clocks, and inkwells

art with themes of balls, balloons, machines,
time, sunsets, or children at school

Water

blue or black fabric, paint, flowers, wall
covering, accessories, doormat, or carpet
undulating-lined designs
glass-top table
swagged curtains
tablecloths
collections grouped together that vary in height
and shape such as dolls, dragons,
and music boxes
artwork with themes of sailing, beach scenes,
swimming, gentle water, children playing,
or clouds
batiks

Wood

green, lime, or turquoise fabric, paint, flowers,
wall covering, accessories, doormat, or
carpet
striped or lined upholstery, window treatments,
or carpeting
four-seater or sectional sofas
pleated curtains
vertical or horizontal blinds
rectangular cocktail table
collections of backgammon boards, vases,
lighthouses, miniature cars, pens, door
knockers, or books
artwork with themes of forests, corn or hay
fields, city scapes, bridges, obelisks, and
ladders

If intimacy and socializing are valuable commodities to you, look carefully at a potential partner's gathering space. Gathering is the act of drawing together, and this room reveals how important social connections are. If little time is spent in a gathering room or little provision is made for comfortable interaction, this individual will not likely be a good candidate with whom to build an intimate home life.

16

DINING AREAS

Where people dine is key to how they feel about themselves. Dining in a kitchen or an area not set up comfortably for dining is throwing away a daily opportunity for satisfaction. Relegating most meals to the kitchen is tantamount to eating lunch at one's desk.

I know a couple, both very busy business executives, who dine formally at home at least once a week. On a selected weekend evening they prepare a gourmet meal, set the table with its finery, light candles, and dress up. Their faithfulness to a ceremonious routine is the underpinning of their mutual respect and a guarantee of meaningful time spent together.

My friend Astrid, a busy interior designer with a husband and two young children, makes the time each day to have her tea poolside. Even though she rarely spends more than ten minutes breakfasting, no matter how busy, she takes appropriate time for herself, and this gesture spills over into all facets of her life. In some ways, one cannot be fully cognizant of a person's feelings without having the ability to honor one's own.

While there are typically only a few official dining areas, there are many other places where it's fun to eat. A breakfast tray in bed, a winter's supper around a fireplace, coffee and dessert by the pool, or punch and cookies in a garden are some ways to turn the ordinary into the remarkable. The very essence of self-worth is often expressed by how solicitous we are to ourselves. As infants we seek to thrive and create as many positive experiences as possible. When self-love is not carried forth through adulthood, one can only assume a lack of self-worth. If you seek someone who has the capacity to be all he or she can be and who can be there cheering you on too, look for someone who will care enough about himself or herself to spend time and energy creating a favorable mealtime ambience.

Entertaining and food are almost synonymous. A dining room's ambience areas are key to understanding how comfortable one is with others. Those who entertain frequently are, more often than not, comfortable with being self-sufficient, and those who avoid it may do so because of feelings of inadequacy.

How a dining room is lit is an indicator of how comfortable one is spending time one on one. When there are no provisions for dimming lights or having illumination only over the dining table, a person may be uncomfortable with intimacy.

Basically, we eat and talk at mealtimes. Up to a point the more furbished and detailed a dining room is, the more stimulating conversation will be. When we encounter stimuli, we become stimulating. When there are few visual, auditory, or olfactory sensations, we are forced to turn inward, which is not the ideal state for communication.

The more detailed a dining room is, the more stimulating conversation will be.

Having a serving area or a place to keep bowls of food, carafes of drink, or excess candles close at hand is a sign that meals are meant to be enjoyed, not just consumed. The more conveniences in a dining room for keeping food warm, drinks filled, and music ongoing, the greater the chances that dining is a favored way to socialize.

Accessories that reflect heritage are especially significant in a dining room. My friend Joyce has a samovar that was brought over from Russia by her grandmother. Her grandmother's home was the bright light in a rather dim childhood. Sundays were the best days of her week, when she visited a sparkling clean home filled with the aromas of baked goods and exotic foods that she learned to love. Her early home life was blighted by her father's early demise and her mother's subsequent economic struggles. It did not strike me as unusual that she chose to pass over her mother's belongings in favor of her grandmother's. Often accessories placed in a dining room will reflect deeply satisfying emotional connections to the past.

Positive Signs in a Dining Room
clean and cared-for dining room table
flexible lighting
rug or carpet

auxiliary surface for serving
accessories from one's past or present generation
candlesticks
fresh flowers
artwork on the walls

Red Flags in a Dining Room (may indicate a lack of desire to nurture oneself and others)

clutter on the table
bright lighting or lighting that cannot be dimmed
windows to street without window covering
cold floors
few accessories
wall art that is difficult to see or positioned too high to see when
    seated

Restaurant owners know that using the color red will stimulate patrons to consume faster. Perhaps those who choose to decorate a dining room with red either don't want guests to linger or want conversation to sparkle. By choosing red, a person is placing value on conversation and entertainment rather than nurturing and caretaking.

The symbols representing elements in a dining room are very telling since food and life are synonymous. How you will be sustained, cared for, and in many ways loved can be suggested by the details in a dining area.

Note how long meals take. Time is a scope-ing factor, especially in a dining room. The more time spent partaking of a meal, the more content one likely is with life.

> **The more time spent at meals, the more likely it is that a person is content.**

COMMON SYMBOLS DISPLAYED IN DINING ROOMS THAT EXPRESS PARTICULAR ELEMENTS

In addition to the color, line, and shape of objects in this area, the following symbols can help you uncover a person's elemental type. Dining areas can express a person's expressed or emotional element, depending on how frequently the person eats there. The less often a person dines at home, the more likely it is that this area will represent his or her expressed element. The more time one spends dining, the more this room represents the hidden element or emotions.

Fire

red or orange colors for fabric, paint, centerpiece, floor covering, window treatment, or artwork
flame-stitch or chevron patterns
Oriental rugs
chandeliers with triangular drop crystals
pyramidal or conical accessories
candles
chairs with spindles protruding above the chair's back

Earth

terra-cotta, deep yellow, or brown fabric, paint, centerpiece, floor covering, window treatment, or artwork
square or checkered designs
club or tufted chairs
square table
cabinet without legs
dark wood furniture
paintings of mountains, land, or beaches

Metal

white, silver, gold, or copper fabric, paint, centerpiece, floor covering, window treatment, or artwork
dots or round circular gestures on designs
brass, silver, or copper chandeliers
round table
round-backed chairs
gold flatware
mirrors
metal trim on plates
paintings of reflected surfaces (still lifes, water, glass buildings)
glossy painted walls or high-polished floors

Water

blue or black fabric, paint, centerpiece, floor
    covering, window treatment, or artwork
sponged walls
glass-top table
swagged curtains
tablecloths to floor
stereo in dining room
artwork with clouds
elaborate chandeliers

Wood

green, lime, or turquoise fabric, paint, center-
    piece, floor covering, window treatment,
    or artwork
striped or linear designs
ladder-backed chairs
rectangular table
pleated curtains
vertical or horizontal blinds
collections of canisters, tall candlesticks
wall candle sconces
artwork of city skyline
grandfather clocks

A person who feels satisfied with life tends to spend time creating a special place to dine. It is the single daily activity that promises contentment. The way a person chooses to use it, abuse it, or ignore it can illuminate how he or she tends to handle other gratification. One who cannot satisfactorily create an agreeable space in which we dine may have little hope of orchestrating ongoing pleasures in life.

17

KITCHENS

A kitchen is the heart of a home. Dwellings originally consisted of a place in which to sleep safely and a location to prepare and eat food. There is no substitute for the aroma, sight, and taste of food. Sophisticated and pristine trappings might make good glossy magazine photographs, but kitchens are best when they are set up to stimulate the senses. Kitchens are laboratories for food preparation, and the more engaged the senses, the more likely one is to enjoy the moment. It may be laughable to think of building a home without a kitchen, but there are some who dust their stove tops because they use them so infrequently. In contrast, those who find joy in cooking often are those who enjoy experimenting, risk taking, and nurturing others.

If the refrigerator is filled with prepackaged foods and the cupboards hold stacks of canned goods, do not expect the owner to be a firebrand of creativity. When a fire or water type, this person has probably cast aside his or her fertile imagination. All elemental types like to cook, but fire relishes experimenting, and water enjoys baking. Pots hanging over a stove, a jar crowded with cooking utensils, or a cupboard jammed with exotic ingredients indicates someone who is likely to be effusive.

> **Those who cook without recipes usually are adventurous in all areas.**

Adults who don't cook may be uncomfortable with experiencing feelings. My friend Lee has had two husbands who did not cook.

Both had difficulty expressing their emotions. If you are looking for a mate who has access to his or her emotional life, look for one who stocks a refrigerator with flair and loves to cook.

I realize many of you may be thinking about sons, boyfriends, or fathers who would not be able to survive a long blizzard if they had to rely on their ability to be inventive in a kitchen. Whether or not people qualify as gourmet cooks is less important than their level of comfort with preparing meals. Time notwithstanding, those who have empty cupboards and don't find the time to cook for themselves as well as others might be more comfortable receiving than giving.

A kitchen is not the optimal place to dine. Just as it is unlikely that you will truly unwind at a desk, it is not normally possible to relax completely when dining next to a food preparation area. Those who do so may see home as a stopping-off point between activities. Reading, listening to the radio, or watching TV during a meal may indicate a discomfort with being alone.

> **Feeding another is the plate on which caring is served.**

A kitchen's energy bespeaks an owner's vitality. Using a kitchen counter as a repository for junk may predict the inability to carry out intentions. A kitchen that seems ignored or is not individualized with accessories reveals a disregard for maintaining good health. I should have been suspicious when my former husband refused to cook a meal even when I was recuperating from surgery. Feeding another is the plate upon which much caring is served. A potential partner who does not cook had better have a very good reason why. Not being involved with a basic life function is at best suspect.

Positive Signs in a Kitchen

clean and tidy
bowl of fresh fruit or flowers
throw rug near sink
display of utensils or pots and pans
herbs (dried or fresh)

cupboards filled with choices of foods

Red Flags in a Kitchen (may indicate a lack of self-esteem or an inability to nurture)

unkempt
soiled dish towels or sponges
unwashed dishes
supermarket bags as trash can or still
    holding groceries
cat's food dishes on countertop
a basically empty refrigerator
cupboards with few selections
cupboards with cases of one or two items
catchall for odds and ends on countertops

COMMON SYMBOLS DISPLAYED IN KITCHENS THAT EXPRESS PARTICULAR ELEMENTS

In addition to the color, line, and shape of objects used in this area, the following symbols reinforce a person's elemental type.

Fire

red or orange fabric, paint, stain, flooring,
    appliances, window treatment, or
    wall covering
chevrons, straight lines, or geometric prints
    on flooring or walls
display of knives
three-legged stools
conical teakettles

Earth

tan, brown, deep gold fabric, paint, stain,
    flooring, appliances, window treatment,
    or wall covering
clay pots
square or chunky canisters
light wood utensils
real or artificial bananas, lemons, or pears

Metal

white, gold, silver, or copper fabric, paint, stain,
  flooring, appliances, window treatment,
  or wall covering
chrome blenders
rounded teakettles
rounded chair backs
shiny or chrome backsplashes
round clocks
globe lights
more than one calendar

Water

blue or black fabric, paint, stain, flooring,
  appliances, window treatment, or wall
  covering
undulating lines in flooring or wall covering
hanging display of glasses or pots and pans
dim lighting

Wood

green or striped fabric, paint, stain, flooring,
  appliances, window treatment, or wall
  covering
more than four appliances on the counter
canning jars
cylindrical canisters
collections of salt and pepper shakers
plants

Without sustenance we wither away and die, and without attention to a room understood to sustain life, a person underscores an
inability to nourish a relationship.

18

BEDROOMS

Bedrooms are private sanctuaries, rooms dissociated from public functions. Western culture sanctions sharing a bedroom with those we feel close to. A bedroom is a safe haven to cry, shout, yelp with joy, and display a full range of emotions. Physical and emotional safety is primary in a bedroom.

A traditional two-story home positions bedrooms upstairs. The location of bedrooms in a single-story house is more haphazard. There does not seem to be an architectural standard shared by contemporary builders. In the Middle East, bedrooms are buried deep in the rear of a home and only family members are allowed in. A Middle Eastern family would no more throw visitors' coats on a master bed than we would serve Thanksgiving dinner from the bedroom. Westerners have a more laissez-faire attitude about bedrooms, and they sometimes double as a family meeting space or entertainment area.

Memory of place refers to what we expect to find in any location. We learn to expect certain standards such as light switches near entrance doors, bathrooms near bedrooms, refrigerators in the kitchen, etc. These are a few norms that when not present baffle and frustrate us. Anything out of the ordinary in a bedroom is even more stressful than it is in other rooms.

Having a childhood bedroom to themselves leaves many adults unable to satisfactorily share this personal space. As adults we are encouraged to mate and form an alliance that includes, in most cases, sharing a bedroom. Understanding how you use this space is key to being able to share it.

Many people lack the skills to share a bedroom.

Perhaps because we are most vulnerable when asleep, where a bed is located can speak volumes about how we approach challenges, fears, and tasks. Jennifer, an owner of a New Age store, confided to me that she slept fitfully at night. When she told me her bed was positioned with its headboard facing away from the entrance door, I was reasonably certain that she felt unprotected at night and could not fall deeply asleep.

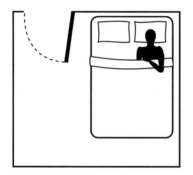

This position is not likely occupied by a take-charge person.

A bed facing away from the door robs its occupant of power.

Since her home's second bedroom has a solid wall across from the entrance door, I suggested she change rooms. Jennifer, like many, continued a routine that didn't serve her, rather than taking charge and changing it. This is a sign of relinquishing the power to influence one's own fate. To march successfully toward a goal requires taking action.

I recently visited the home of a jeweler in West Virginia. Since she was in her early fifties and had never been married, I was searching for a sign that would reveal her lack of desire to form a long-term intimate relationship. She had never been without intimate male companionship and claimed she wanted to be married, so why she was not was even more baffling. It was only when I entered her bedroom that I saw a clue. She had placed her bed facing away from the entrance door, tucking it behind a rather tall dresser. When in bed, her view of her bedroom's entrance was obstructed, suggesting she was fearful and would retreat from instead of confront problems. I suggested she move the bed to the other wall and position a mirror high enough to see the door but not herself, thereby helping her squarely face the door, which is a metaphor for facing other issues.

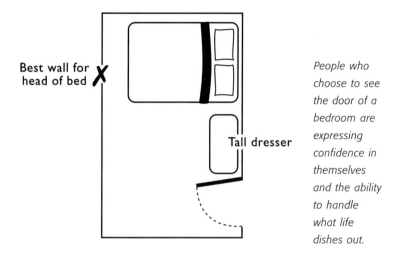

Best wall for head of bed ✗

Tall dresser

People who choose to see the door of a bedroom are expressing confidence in themselves and the ability to handle what life dishes out.

On which side of the bed does a person sleep? Whether alone or with another, the person who sleeps closest to the door or at the best angle to see anyone who enters bears the most responsibility.

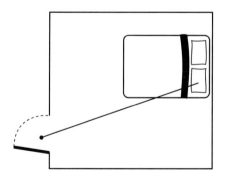

The person who sleeps here is likely to assume responsibilities in a relationship.

Sleeping farthest from an entrance door may indicate fear of assuming responsibilities.

If you become involved with someone who sleeps tucked away from an entrance's view or farthest from the door, you might have to bear the greatest emotional, financial, or social responsibilities. On the other hand, one who sleeps in what feng shui calls the *guardian position* (closest to the door) is one you can count on.

Take note if part of a bed's surface is used as a tabletop. I had a client who after separating from her husband used his side of the bed as a place to pile reading materials. About a year later I noticed that she had created a space for these books elsewhere. This change heralded a new era in her life, and in a relatively short period of time she met a man with whom she became involved.

Benjamin slapped his apartment's floor plans down on my desk one day with the declaration that he wanted to get married. Handsome, intelligent, and successful, there was no reason he would have trouble finding a potential mate. After querying him, I discovered that every dresser, cabinet, and closet in his whole apartment was filled to capacity. How could a relationship enter his life when there was no physical space for another person? I suggested he empty a bureau, clear off a few bookshelves, and vacate part of a closet. Since relationships are give-and-take, making room for another person can be a first step. We must empty to be filled.

> **A person whose home has no empty closets, bureau drawers, or desk drawers is not ready to share his or her life with another.**

Those whose bedroom is like a monk's cell may feel isolated and deprived and could be prone to loneliness. Over and over again in my practice I see that those who do not surround themselves with comforts suffer from a vague sense of emptiness and ennui. One client freely admitted that she did not like to socialize and led a contented, solitary life. Her bedroom, a room with windows on three sides, had no curtains to block the penetrating New England winter sun. A light beige area carpet covered a golden-tone wood floor. A bed, a solitary nightstand, and a highboy were the room's only accoutrements. When a bedroom feels sparse and austere, economics notwithstanding, the capacity for forming enthusiastic, exuberant relationships is more than likely absent.

On the other hand, a bedroom filled with all sorts of extraneous things can consume energy, thwart motivation, and camouflage feelings. It is hard to reach our emotional center when we crowd an area intended as a haven for replenishment.

Is a television set in the bedroom used as an entertainment feature for relaxing or as an escape? The size of the television can offer an answer as can its position. The following are signs that television might be watched too frequently. If two or more answers are yes, you are most probably in the company of a person who uses this as a vehicle for escape. The question to ask then is what they are escaping.

Signs That a TV Is Watched Frequently

comfortable seating especially with an ottoman across from
    the TV set
a TV set with little else surrounding it
a cleared path to the TV set from the bedroom's entrance
insufficient lighting next to the bed
remote control on the nightstand
the TV set directly across from the bed

A bedroom can reveal much personal information. The following guide can be used to help you translate your observations. Be alert to decipher the eccentric or unusual, for whatever flies in the face of convention should be noted. A jeweler friend has a 400-pound steel combination-lock safe in his bedroom. This coupled with the fact that he has been uninvolved for more than ten years leads one to the rather obvious conclusion that he is quite protective of his personal possessions or even his physical and emotional valuables. Don't ignore quirky signs in any room, especially in the bedroom.

Positive Signs in a Bedroom

made-up bed
tidy dresser top
adequate lighting on both sides of the bed
window coverings that both let in light and provide privacy
comforter at edge of bed or on a chair
candles

Red Flags in a Bedroom (*may indicate a desire to distance oneself from others or a lack of power to orchestrate life*)

unkempt bed
work-related materials on nightstand
single chair

TV directly across from the bed
too many furnishings
musty smell
no photographs or personal icons
more than one clock

Common Symbols Displayed in Bedrooms That Express Particular Elements

In addition to the color, line, and shape of objects used in this area, the following symbols can reinforce a person's elemental type. The symbols expressed in a bedroom reveal one's hidden or emotional element.

Fire

red or orange fabric, paint, bed covering, window treatment, wall covering, or carpet
chevrons, straight lines, or geometric prints
conical lamp shades
sconces
four-poster bed without side bars on top
geometric or hard-edged paintings

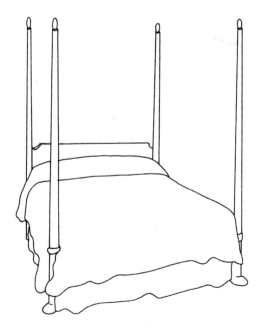

A four-poster bed without upper railings typically represents the fire element.

Earth

tan, brown, deep gold fabric, paint, bed
   covering, window treatment, wall covering,
   or carpet
footboard
chair without legs or pedestal
skirted nightstand
pleated skirt on box spring
extremely fluffy comforter
chest at end of bed
landscape or paintings with large objects

Metal

white, gold, silver, or copper fabric, paint, bed
   covering, window treatment, wall covering,
   or carpet
oval or round area carpet
sheer curtains
round-back chair or headboard
shiny-surfaced desk
abstract expressionist or pointillist-style painting
more than two telephones
globe light

Water

blue or black fabric, paint, bed covering,
   window treatment, wall covering, or carpet
white-noise mechanism
a great many bed pillows
indoor recirculating fountain
tufted upholstery
enclosure for TV
seascape paintings or ones with undulating lines
draped fabric on window or four-poster bed
curved or intricately lined headboard

Wood

green fabric, paint, bed covering, window
   treatment, wall covering, or carpet
tall or leggy dresser or wardrobe
spindle-legged desk

bookcase
columns or vertical lines on headboard
a painting of many trees or high-rise buildings

Icons placed in a bedroom reveal what we deem valuable and shine a light into the deepest reaches of a soul. Feng shui wisdom suggests that when a relationship is over the bedroom must be altered. Fresh sheets, coverlets, and even a new bed are suggested to reclaim the space. It is easy to see that reminders of an old relationship can be damaging when desirous of forming new ones. When a relationship is over, it is important to reassert one's identity and recapture a space to clear the way for renewal. A bedroom is a good place to start when change is desired. Change one thing in your bedroom and see how your life is affected.

19

BATHROOMS

Nothing is quite so cloistered as time spent in a bathroom. For the most part, it is acceptable to lock the door and not be disturbed. When we are exposed physically, we are likely to feel more vulnerable and insecure. How we choose to view and amend our perceived assets or imperfections tells a great deal about us. In this most private, secluded setting deeply personal revelations can be gleaned by an astute observer.

I have a friend who lets nothing stand in the way of her succeeding. An unusual aspect of her home is that there is no mirror above her bathroom sink. When I asked her why, she replied that she would rather look out a window or at one of the framed art pieces hanging on the walls than gaze at her face under bright lights. After all, she went on, there are so many more interesting things to look at than herself brushing her teeth. Those who reduce all potentially undermining conditions at home are their own best allies. Characteristically those who feel good about themselves are likely to excel.

My dear mother is a hypochondriac, and to my knowledge rarely a month passes without a visit to one of the army of physicians who attend her. The slightest abdominal pang, the smallest hint of congestion sends her into a tornado of action. Her medicine chest looks like the restocking shelf for a pharmacy, while my dad's restorative needs are represented by a single bottle of pills with an expired date. On Mom's side of the sink's counter are bottles and canisters filled with health aids. Cotton swabs for applying ointments, diminutive drinking cups to help down pills, and an assortment of travel containers to hold her most recent curative are perched on a tray as if their movement to bedside is imminent. No need to be a rocket scientist to figure out that she is either very sick or worries about being sick. Fortunately, the latter is true, but her addiction to apprehension is easy to see when surveying her bathroom.

Many years ago, when I traveled to Washington, D.C., to sell my art, I stayed at a patron's home. During a tour of the home I was taken to a bathroom where a desk had been installed for the husband's use. No matter what the constraints of space are, any significant part of one's life, other than normal bathroom activities, conducted in a bathroom is not a good sign. In this case the husband was hoping to open his own plumbing business, and the fact that it never came to pass comes as no surprise The lack of an esteemed place for the office indicated the couple did not hold the husband's talents in high regard.

A positive bathroom

A bathroom with red flags

For the most part, the time we invest in caring for ourselves mirrors our capacity to care for others. Too much or too little can be a source of concern and represent potential sources of aggravation later on. Albert Einstein comes to mind when conjuring up someone who appeared not to care about grooming. Pictures reveal him with hair askew, tie disheveled, sweater rumpled, and suit ill fitting. After reading his biography, I realized he lived entirely for his work and had little capacity for personal relationships and little interest in personal grooming. He appeared to have married women who didn't do much more than serve his domestic needs. Although he is held in esteem for his genius and capacity to uncover scientific phenomenon, he was clearly deficient in intimacy, his own and with others. I suspect his bathroom was not filled with many personal grooming aids.

On a more personal note, another friend has a glass-top table across from her toilet with all kinds of reading materials. I delight in thinking about her catching up on her reading while otherwise disposed. She certainly is a dynamo, one who doesn't like to miss anything. In fact, many of her friends call her affectionately their "time efficiency expert." Had I not known her, the rather unusual table piled high with books in that location would have told me that she is not one to waste time.

Bachelors tend to neglect bathrooms. Men usually have fewer grooming needs than women. As a matter of fact, for me it would be a red flag if I were to visit the home of a single male whose bathroom looked like it was modeled after a room in the Taj Mahal. Too much attention to physical care can denote either insecurity or self-centeredness.

Scope-ing a bathroom doesn't require much because certain fixtures are preplaced.

Positive Signs in the Bathroom Typically Used for Grooming

tidy
clean towels
throw rug over tile or linoleum floor
grooming aids
magazines or books
candles
aromatics

Red Flags in Bathroom Typically Used for Grooming (may indicate a lack of self-esteem or an inability to nurture)

unkempt
towels or clothes on floor
no soap dish
no toilet paper holder
no wall decorations
no shower curtain
overflowing laundry
foul smelling
more than two mirrors or two mirrored walls

COMMON SYMBOLS DISPLAYED IN BATHROOMS THAT EXPRESS PARTICULAR ELEMENTS

In addition to the color, line, and shape of objects used in this area, the following symbols can reinforce a person's elemental type. The symbols expressed in a bathroom reveal a person's emotional element.

Fire

red or bright orange triangular candles, towels, soaps, floor mat, window treatment, or shower curtain and toiletry holders
chevrons, straight lines, or geometric prints
conical lights
vertical toothbrush holder including toothbrush

Earth

oranges, browns, or deep gold square candles, towels, soaps, floor mat, window treatment, or shower curtain and toiletry holders
dim lighting
a great many bottles on a counter or back of a toilet
wicker wastepaper basket or clothes hamper
ceramic planters or holders for toothpaste, soap, etc.
wooden or fabric toilet seat cover

Metal

white, gray, silver, gold, or copper round candles, towels, soaps, floor mat, window treatment, or shower curtain and toiletry holders
white walls with little artwork, many mirrors
gold or silver frames and accessories
round floor mat
theatrical dressing room lighting
books or artwork to read
toilet paper cover

Water

blue or black amorphous candles, towels, soaps, floor mat, window treatment, or shower curtain and toiletry holders

dissimilar towels

curved- or wavy-patterned shower curtain or window treatment

many plants

radio or facility for music

Wood

green towels, rectangular candles, towels, soaps, floor mat, window treatment, or shower curtain and toiletry holders

striped shower curtain, towels with horizontal trim, tall cylinders for toothbrush holders

standing towel rack

Part IV

FURNITURE STYLES

O ne story of a culture is told through the imagination and talent of artisans who translate the prevailing philosophy, taste, style, and social conditions into aesthetic forms. Furniture design is no less an art form than painting and sculpture; the only difference is its utilitarian objective. A whole host of influences is mirrored in the look and feel of furniture. Wars, alliances, and trade make an indelible imprint on a culture, as do architectural innovations and interest in decorative art forms. Use, however, is governed by social customs, dress, geographical conditions, and class, and each period has particular needs that are served by interior furnishings.

When a style is reinterpreted in a later era, it often transcends its original purpose, and its choice is no longer based on utility or custom but on personal preferences. As such it represents an important aspect of the person who chose it. Take for example, a Spanish vargueno, which is a hinged wooden drop-front cabinet that sits atop a table and was designed as a receptacle for documents and valuables. Today reproductions of varguenos are made to be storage units for televisions, stemware, stereos, and minibars. A person who selects this kind of furniture designed for portability is in some ways expressing a flexibility that opens the door to letting others enter.

Although it is fascinating to understand why a style of furniture emerged and what made its expression timely and acceptable, it is not within the scope of this book to delve into such a complete history of furniture. There is, however, a spirit of the times related to an elemental characteristic expressed in any piece. Those who choose to live with that style today are expressing some form of that elemental spirit.

The style of furniture selected reveals beliefs, values, and elemental characteristics of a person.

Each chapter in Part IV will cover a particular period of decoration and decor. Each period has features that favor one element over the others. Even if you do not see the specific furniture style in a home, you may see portions of a style that can help you identify the element of a particular piece of furniture. The aim is to give you another tool to assist in deciphering the elements expressed in a home.

20

SPANISH STYLE: GEOMETRIC DETAILS AND PORTABILITY

W hat is so distinctive about Spanish furniture between the eighth century and the late sixteenth century is the influence of two cultures. In the eighth century the Spanish people were conquered by the Islamic Moors from Africa across the Strait of Gibraltar. The Christians who had dominated the culture up until that point were pushed aside only to regain their hold at the end of the fifteenth century. This seven-century rule by the Moors produced a unique decorative style, one that merged the aesthetics of two worlds.

Since the Moors' religious principles forbade representational forms of humans, animals, and plants, these followers of Muhammad became the world's finest geometricians and employed an endless variety of geometric designs and patterns in all their decorative arts. Those who are not aficionados of contemporary art can choose a replica of this style to display geometric forms, which in most cases express the metal element.

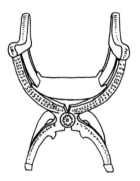

The two arched members give this chair a metal expression. Moreover, this folding chair expresses metal's reduction capacity.

A distinctive Spanish-style chair represents the element metal, for many reasons: Most chairs have four legs planted underneath the seat's four corners. Although the Spanish were not the first to conceptualize a chair or stool folding by means of a cross member, the Spanish version has been the most frequently reinterpreted. The central pin supporting the frame gives this chair an air of vulnerability and impermanence, and the frontal view has a stronger line than the details. Merely looking at this chair can provoke an urge to swoop it up and move it to another location. Since the supports, when viewed from the front, are shaped like two scooped-out circles, the chair takes on metal's shape. Also, since metal encourages rethinking ideas, actions, etc., anything that urges you to shift perception incorporates metal's bias. Therefore, furniture with the metal element tends to be portable.

A person choosing metal's quality implies a willingness to make changes and can in fact be revealing dissatisfaction with his or her present state. Those who choose this style often are ready to make a commitment to a relationship because they are expressing ease with altering their life.

Another interesting feature of this chair is the leather sling serving as the seat. The unsupported leather seat stretches when sat on and gives the user a feeling of being held by the chair. After sitting on this leather sling for only a short while, the feeling of support gives way to feeling trapped, and one's natural tendency is to want to get up. Feeling slightly cramped, one is inclined to think about this situation if only to make the decision to get up. The element metal is aligned with making measured decisions, encouraging thoughtfulness, not impulsiveness. Therefore, any seating that gives way and makes it difficult to rise suggests that this person is not about to make an impulsive decision but will mull it over carefully. A person who chooses this kind of seating will not likely ask you to elope.

The wooden cabinets called varguenos, also typical of this period, were designed to be lifted and moved from location to location. Much Spanish furniture of the eighth through the late sixteenth centuries in fact appears portable. One who is not settled in life is likely to select furnishings that are lightweight and easy to transport because he or she has not found that sense of permanence that makes one want to be settled.

The trestle table's distinctive feature is the spindly or spiral-shaped legs. Round shapes and patterns and highly polished surfaces force the eye to move or react and are typical of metal's characteristics. One who opts for the round and circular shapes that keep the eyes moving likes to be engaged mentally. If you see a trestle table's leg shape, be sure to keep your end of a conversation sparkling.

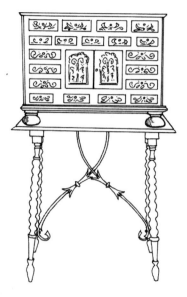

Those who are still searching for a relationship are likely to purchase lightweight, transportable furnishings.

Spiral-shaped legs release the mental spin of metal's proclivity.

When a piece of furniture has a prominent round medallion, we are being asked to give that person our undivided attention.

Details force us to focus. Any furniture or accessory that draws us in to observe it closely gives off one of metal's messages, which is to pay attention. In the same way as jogging without paying careful attention to small changes on a road's surface can be catastrophic, lack of focus on the minute aspects of this person's life can herald the end of the relationship.

Categorize accessories or furnishings that use the physical gestures described in this chapter, as metal. Choosing the metal element implies one is open to change, wants to be involved intensely, and needs to have another's undivided attention. It can also support a desire to be aligned with both the exotic and the mysterious. Those who travel extensively to experience differences or who would like to, find themselves drawn to furnishings that have many metal elements.

21

LOUIS XIV AND XV: CURVED LINES AND ABUNDANT DETAILS

D uring the reign of Louis XIV and Louis XV the decorative arts contributed to the glorification of the state and reflected the king's influence. This style is laden with sumptuous detail and exaggerated and dramatic movement. Its lines most often expressed flights of fancy, carvings surging and rippling through a variegated thickness of polished wood. Those choosing to live with such a diverse array of swooping lines and gestures are likely to feel out of sync with today's spare lines and want to be transported, as Alice in Wonderland was, to a land of outrageous magic. To intrigue this type, be as dramatic and mysterious as you possibly can. Rational explanations leave people who make these choices cold. They prefer intrigue and mystery. Leave unsigned notes and gifts on their doorstep.

Rippling details suggest the water element.

Classical references inspired details, and exotic materials were used to showcase techniques that today have no equal. Surfaces were enriched by marquetry, which required metal and tortoiseshell to be inlaid onto tops of wood furniture. Almost impossible to duplicate today because of the enormous amount of labor required, this furniture style is marked by an abundance of detailing.

The fluidity of an ocean with its rising and falling waves seems to radiate from the carved wood details, and the push and pull of the marquetry surfaces express many of water's elemental qualities.

Those selecting furniture that requires close inspection are clamoring to be appreciated. Water types feel that others miss the rich depth of their feelings. Selecting a piece of furniture that requires others to focus on details is in some ways what they are imploring you to do with them.

Seating low to the ground traps you, as does the water element.

Most of us can bounce up from a seat as long as it is not too close to the floor. A wide, low chair, however, like those characteristic of this period and style, restricts movement—as does water. Deep or low seating suggests a desire to form a meaningful relationship, to seduce those who sit down. Those who do not want others to stick around will choose seats that are easy to get out of. Trying to move through water can make us feel trapped, and so can sitting in a low seat. If you are not interested in the person whose seating is low and wide, don't toy with his or her emotions. Because they want emotional connections, if they believe you do too, they might be hard to disengage from.

This style forces us to pay attention to either feeling or concealing. This choice suggests a person who may be overbearing. An abundance of this kind of water element suggests focusing too much on one's emotional life.

22

CHIPPENDALE, ADAM, AND HEPPLEWHITE FURNITURE

Cabinetmakers Chippendale, Adam, and Hepplewhite were responsible for a decorative style that closed the door on an era of ornately carved, heavy furniture. Stirred by classic styles of the Chinese, Greeks, and Romans, their furniture became popular during the times surrounding the French and American revolutions (1750–90). By spurning art forms favored by old regimes, those favoring a change in the order of the day could identify with a style that represented a new world order. Favoring these pivotal styles, generally known as *neoclassicism*, can indicate one who is ready to make changes and willing to accept new vistas.

Although these styles had distinctly different details, they are grouped together in this book because they frequently used the fire element. Fire enhances the desire as well as acceptance for change. Whether triangles are created by an overall shape, by negative space, or applied as an embellishment, accepting a fire symbol in furniture styling suggests that one is comfortable with a certain degree of instability and is willing to move away from the past.

All of these artisans had a knowledge of and appreciation for past designs and produced an amazing number of styles and forms. The furniture depicted here does not in any way represent all their efforts, only those pieces that show how a triangle, representing the element fire, is used successfully in furniture design.

When you are in the presence of one who chooses furnishings and accessories with the triangular line and the color red, you are with someone who may be full of surprises, is likely to take action rather than be passive, and has a great deal of energy, be it physical, emotional, or intellectual.

THOMAS CHIPPENDALE (1718–79)

Although historians argue that Chippendale was given credit for practically every fine piece of mahogany furniture made in England during his era, he himself probably never carved at all.

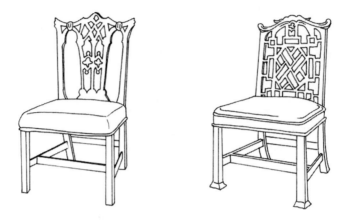

Chairs with many triangular elements are aligned with the fire element.

Observe the top of the backs of chairs and note how they sweep past the edge of the two adjoining sections. This gesture reminds one of the point at the end of an elf's hat. Creating a tiny triangle at the chair's back gives the impression of movement, as does a flickering flame. Even the squares and rectangles used in these chairs are positioned in such a way as to give the impression of an X, which captures the look of an actual and inverted flame. This line feels unstable, as can a person who chooses furnishings with a fire element.

The overall shape of a mirror takes precedence over the details because the largest surface, the mirror itself, is distracting to the eye.

Since most of us are observing ourselves when close to a mirror, its outline takes precedence over its details. The illustrated Chippendale mirror exemplifies this; the details are formed by water's wavy lines, but the shape is an inverted arrow, which is fire.

A fire type who wants to be noticed often selects double triangles or lattice designs on furniture's surfaces.

A lattice creates repetitive triangles and draws the eye in, as does the fire element. Since the diagonal line is the least frequently used line in furnishings and since it is so compelling (try *not* looking at it), the person who selects latticework in a furniture design may need to be the center of attention.

ROBERT ADAM (1728–92)

Adam, an Englishman, came from a family of architects and designers, not cabinetmakers, and was influenced by his visit to the recently excavated ruins of Pompeii. After returning to England, he fused what he saw with his personal vision. The results were astounding and almost instantly accepted. Adam's influence completely penetrated architecture and was the final death blow for the ornate rococo style.

The lightweight pedestal illustrated here looks like a triangle. Note the smaller triangle down the middle, reinforcing this shape as well as the structure. People who pick an inverted flame are trying to hold their fiery aspects in check. If the person you are trying to get to know doesn't appear to have the personality of fire, dig deeper into the person's emotional life to discover which of fire's qualities his or her emotions have. In fact, one who favors any inverted shape is usually trying to repress or hide something.

Almost flamelike, this pedestal uses a triangle to keep it from leaping up visually.

A three-dimensional detail on a piece often categorizes its element. The fluid overall shape takes a backseat to the distinctive V-shaped rope encircling the urn pictured.

The raised rope design encircling the urn lends a fire element to this piece.

Unfolded wings look like triangles and feel tenuous and unstable like the fire element. Even the rather ponderous cabinet pictured is lightened with the detail of the wings. Whenever wings are dominant, the piece falls into a fire category.

Consider pieces with distinctive wings as fire elements.

Choosing wings as a dominant detail is similar to having a fascination for angels. Both wings and angels can lift us metaphorically out of the mundane, and people who favor these symbols often feel as if their life is not as charmed as they wish it to be. Giving them hope and some ideal to grasp is a surefire way to win their friendship.

GEORGE HEPPLEWHITE (D. 1786)

While little precise information exists about George Hepplewhite, his name is given to a particular furniture style in vogue from 1780 to 1795. He fashioned a leg that flares from the floor and sometimes is embellished with fluting or incising.

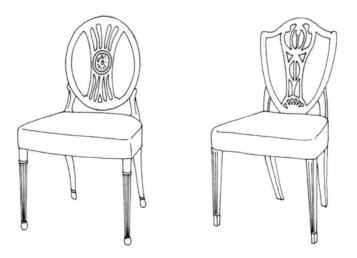

A tapered leg looks like an inverse flame.

A tapered leg is fragile, as are all objects subjected to fire's devastating effect. Selecting a chair that rests on the narrowest part of the entire design can signify vulnerability. Be certain to do what you say with this person, or he or she will cringe away from you like a single strand of hair does when it is held over a flame.

Choosing this bench with its heart-shaped back is like
wearing your heart on your sleeve.

The design of the illustrated bench represents fire at its most vulnerable. Although there are many triangular shapes, the overall fluidity of the chair back's heart shape mixes the elements fire and water and exposes a feeling of vulnerability. Be gentle and careful with this person in matters of the heart. He or she is thin skinned and easily hurt.

Even though you may not see furniture exactly like the ones in this chapter, look for the suggestion of fire through the overall shape, use of diagonal lines, prominent detail, tapered legs, or wings.

23

VICTORIAN AND ART NOUVEAU: CONSTRAINED LINES GIVE WAY TO FLUID ONES

VICTORIAN

The Victorian period (roughly 1815–1900) was filled with revivals and interpretations of many styles. With the emergence of the industrial age, the refined lines gave way to coarser ones. A thickening of form and a reduction of sparseness returned furniture's look to a more solid look. With so many changes thrust on a society, it is no wonder that an aesthetic evolved that articulated earth's safety and stability. Restrictive clothing made moving frivolously strenuous, and indoor life felt stodgy and immutable, like challenged earth.

Victorian chairs exude a sturdy earthbound look.

Those who choose furnishings with ornate earth elements are apt to be controlling. If you are a free spirit, be wary of their desire to keep you on a predictable course.

239

Not all Victorian furniture replicates earth's form and line. At a time when no one knew what changes the Industrial Revolution would bring, Victorian furnishings incorporated all possibilities. American Victorian style incorporates all periods, mixed indiscriminately.

The top detail likens this Victorian chair to fire and the sturdy squared-off bottom to earth.

Those who bring a fire/earth element into a home want to be in a relationship, with a self-sufficient partner. Be alert to their needs, for while they might seem full of energy, they do need a lot of downtime.

This dresser's chunky, heavy look exudes earth's stability or stubbornness. When a home is filled with a preponderance of furniture with the earth line, stubbornness can be predicted. With only a few pieces stability is more likely.

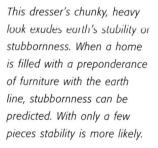

This dining table's round top (signifying metal) is coupled with a chunky earth base.

A person choosing a round table with an earth base often feels as if life is out of control. Whether this seems true to you or not, it is important to soothe rather than excite the person. Plan quiet evenings at home rather than late evenings on the town.

The valance's swag and the curtain's drape are fluid, like water, while the drape ends in a triangular fire shape at the floor, making this a water/fire combination.

Feeling misunderstood by others, a person selecting the window treatment illustrated needs to be coaxed to reveal his or her feelings. The combination of two catalysts means the person is likely to be more comfortable having you make the decisions than figuring out what he or she wants.

Wood's tall rectangles are represented nicely in the leggy Victorian desk, making this an earth/wood combination.

People who choose pieces with both earth and wood are a delight to be with. While they find life's changes invigorating, they are magnets to others because they exude strength.

Art Nouveau

Once the changes of the Industrial Revolution were integrated into society, the earth line of the Victorian gave way to a casual free-flowing organic form. While art nouveau is a group of different movements, it does have some threads of consistency. Abstract, almost floral lines spill across fascias, and supporting members join a dizzying conglomeration of whiplashed lines. Like large waves crashing onto the shores, great crests of lines sweep away the past and make room for new directions. Those choosing this dramatic water line are ready to fight any demons in their way as they head into unknown territory. Fearless and forceful, lovers of art nouveau adore the spirit of leisure and indulge themselves in a mélange of sensuous pleasures.

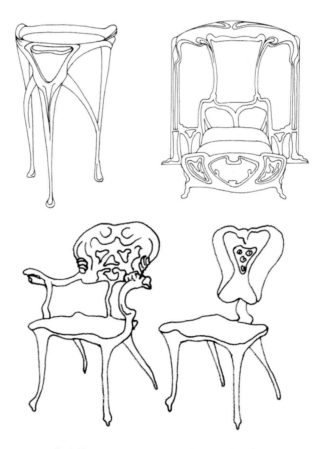

Fluid like water, art nouveau furniture is often chosen by one who loves sensual stimulation.

24

CONTEMPORARY FURNISHINGS: IMAGES HERETOFORE UNKNOWN

Sweeping away visual clutter, the modern movement rejected ornamentation and gave preference to clean lines and pleasing proportions. Although the term *modern* is rather pretentious since all movements deal in the present and hence are contemporary, the designers of the twentieth century had technology heretofore unknown with which to work. New materials spurred the inventive human spirit to come up with entirely new looks.

Typical of the new materials were molded plastics, which gave rise to unusual amorphous forms. Tough new synthetic fibers could be glued and stretched instead of stitched and stuffed. Machinery that could manipulate steel, foam, fiber, plastic, and wood in unique ways gave designers opportunities to experiment. The results were astounding, and the look of contemporary furnishings revolutionized shape and form.

The twentieth century spans a remarkable bridge. Ninety-five years ago my grandparents lived without electricity and traveled in horse-driven carriages for hours to reach a town twenty miles away. Today we can reach anywhere on the planet within minutes on the Internet. Information that is generated in Paris, London, and New York can be viewed in remote Guatemalan villages, and the handicrafts of remote villagers grace pages of catalogs and stores all over the world. There is no style, ornamentation, or design that is not familiar to almost anyone, anywhere.

What has the worldwide information highway wrought in interior design? For one, global access to all art forms and furnishings.

No one would be shocked to walk into a home today and see a sofa covered in an ancient-styled Oriental fabric next to a molded plastic pedestal table on which sits an English carriage-inspired lamp. Sticking to one style is less likely in a world fueled by global aesthetics.

However, two dominant contemporary styles have emerged: Danish modern, which uses the straight rectangular lines of wood, and the formed, stretched water shapes as seen in Olivier Mourgue's furniture in the film *2001: A Space Odyssey*.

Choosing the dramatic water lines of this contemporary furniture suggests comfort with drama and histrionics. A person choosing this style might tend to be melodramatic.

Those choosing the rectangular spare lines of Danish modern furniture articulate wood's characteristic growth and change.

The modern era began after World War I, and perhaps for the first time the preponderance of interior furnishings was developed not for the aristocracy but for the average person. The Danes, Finns, Norwegians, and Swedes, known for their egalitarian political philosophy, sought to make furniture for people who lived ordinary lives. Seeking to incorporate the best of their hand-crafted traditions and natural resources, the Scandinavians produced clean-lined, functional wood furniture. The use of laminates brought the cost and weight of furniture into a modest range.

In an age of new ideas, actions, and horizons the spare rectangular wood line, like the sunrise or spring, connotes beginnings. Scandinavian furnishings signaled the age of the element wood.

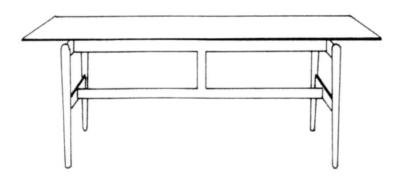

Selecting the clean, unencumbered wood line, sparse of detail, indicates one who is comfortable with communicating straightforwardly.

As the century wore on, slowly, under the influence of Marcel Breuer, beginning in the 1920s, and Charles Eames in the 1940s, the sleek, oscillating, pendulous swing of the water and metal contemporary line unfolded. By the time I worked in the Decoration and Design Building in New York City in the 1960s, the technology of molded plastic had given rise to a whole new look in furnishings. A tapered plastic cylinder lifts this chair seat off the ground, giving it the look of foam riding the crest of a wave.

The fragile water element suggested by this Plexiglas chair by Estelle and Erwine Laverne might be chosen by one who is courageous and not impeded by difficulties.

The Long Chair produced by Airborne International of France expressed the merging of speed and water even more clearly. This silhouette suggests one who is comfortable bypassing the status quo. Visually this water and metal combination produces a stunning rippling effect, and those who like this combination are not likely to be glued to the conventional.

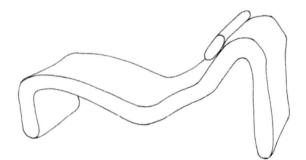

Choosing a piece of furniture like this Long Chair suggests one who is not afraid to step outside mainstream thinking.

Today, as the century comes to a close, a delight in eclecticism combined with the popularity of collecting endows the contemporary interior with an individuality unknown in our brief history on this planet. Being able to create a unique personal setting allows those of us in the twentieth century to display our individuality more than was ever possible before. Someone who passes up this opportunity may not be in touch with his or her inner core. A home without unique features suggests someone who is still struggling with becoming.

Part v

SCOPE-ING INDIVIDUAL PIECES OF FURNITURE

Seating, storing, dining, and sleeping are the requirements that furnishings need to satisfy. However, in each category the variety is endless. The way a piece serves its purpose and its comfort level are two important considerations but not necessarily the most important ones.

Inherent in any action are choices. There are distinctly different ways an activity can be accomplished. For example, one can walk at a leisurely pace, taking time to partake of all sensory experiences, or one can stride swiftly, focusing on little else but reaching a destination. Are these the same experience? Yes and no. Walking requires the use of our legs no matter what the pace or intention, but the way walking is accomplished can vary widely. The same is certainly true of choosing a highboy or shelves in a closet for storing clothes.

Fear and uncertainty can be likened to fire, as can inventiveness and risk taking. Security and stability are aspects of the earth element, as are obstinacy and rebelliousness. One can be refined or withdrawn and express metal's attributes. Being flexible and easygoing are one side of water, as is being persistent. Wood people are often inventive and goal oriented or can be fickle and superficial. On which side of an elemental coin a person lies can be deduced from the visual messages given by various objects.

The unstable shape is reminiscent of a flickering flame and might be selected by one who is not afraid of taking risks.

A fragile triangular vase with its narrow point at the base can elicit a sense of fear, which is associated with fire. A chunky, primitive chest with thick wooden members is rock solid like earth. We select objects not just for their use but because they make us feel a certain way or express what we are feeling. We might want to stash our treasures safely in an earth chest and/or create drama around a display of roses given to us by a lover. We perch on a stool or vegetate on a lounge because these acts support how we choose to live.

Scope-ing specific furniture can give us additional information about another human being. The following chapters will dissect major groups of furniture and how they represent who we are. With apologies to Gertrude Stein, a chair is not just a chair.

25

THE CHAIR

N o single item of furniture has been so used, interpreted, corrupted, or necessary as the chair. From sitting unmanageable children in corners to ensconcing royalty on thrones, humans have used rocks, stumps, and slings and have gilded, carved, tufted, and upholstered them for seating. Chairs help us attend to tasks, socialize, and relax. The first human to create a chair probably found it safer resting above the ground, for it is faster to stand up from above ground zero.

What kind of chair we choose for an activity communicates how we feel about the activity. Stools are perfect examples. Not meant for lounging, a stool requires us to be alert lest we fall from its perch. When there is a task to be attended to that requires a certain amount of alertness, the stool is a perfect choice. Dining on stools around a kitchen counter indicates meals are pragmatic affairs to quell hunger, not social events to encourage conversation. Most stools are leggy and express the wood element. Since mealtimes are often our only daily social time, those who choose to dine on stools are probably not willing to connect with another in an absorbing, intimate way.

I once had a client who motioned me to sit on a footstool placed next to her sofa while we discussed her needs. As I listened to her speak, I realized I would have a difficult time convincing her to follow my solutions. The results were as I feared, and this client had objections to all my recommendations. Sitting me down on a low stool was the first clue that she wanted to devalue my expertise to ignore my advice.

Important socializing does not take place while seated on a stool.

Swivel chairs allow a person to have much more contact with the surroundings, either actively or passively. The metal element is associated with a spinning movement; therefore, swivel chairs are elementally metal. There is no middle ground when choosing a chair that swivels. Whether it is a desk, reading, or dining chair, those who choose swivel chairs are likely to be on the go either physically or mentally. In either case those who prefer swivel chairs are not likely to be stodgy, stubborn, or static.

The following chairs are categorized by their elemental line. When selecting furniture we are likely to select an element that either expresses ourselves deeply or balances parts we feel are missing. For example, a person who does not linger intellectually or physically might select the formed steel wire chair designed by Harry Bertoia for Knoll Associates.

Choosing the crossed lines of Harry Bertoia's chair for Knoll indicates a person who does not like to engage in long conversations and will be more likely to throw large galas than intimate dinner parties.

The crossed lines of the Bertoia chair do not entice one to linger. Chairs with diagonal lines forming triangles exude an energy not unlike a type A personality. Therefore, those who select this seating indicate preferences for brief, stimulating encounters and events.

The rocker has its genesis in the need for movement. Those of us who have been privileged to have children know that a good way to calm an infant is by rocking. The origin of the rocker may have been to assist soothing infants. In any case, a rocker invites you to sit down and stay and while doing so tranquilizes and relaxes. Rocking is a quintessential water experience, and furnishing a home with this chair indicates a water elemental proclivity.

I have a friend who chose a rocking chair that looked perfectly balanced but when sat on swooped backward to what felt like a precariously dangerous place until it returned to its upright position. Sometimes a rocking chair looks unsteady, such as the pictured wrought-iron rocking chair made at the Trenton Iron Works about 1860. The seat looks so much heavier than the base that only the undaunted would venture to sit down without caution.

Be on your toes with a person who chooses a rocker that throws you off balance; this person is likely to surprise you in other ways too.

So long as there is no difference between how a rocker appears and how it functions, water is its elemental experience and the line of the chair is the secondary one. However, when a rocker looks safe but surprises you by tipping over too far, the resulting experience changes the element to fire.

The most interesting phenomenon about a chair is that when seated in it, for the most part, the body obscures its shape. Therefore the main experience of a chair is upon approaching it. Because of the diagonal lines meeting in Xs, the fire element of the illustrated dining room chair stimulates the appetite upon entering a dining room, but when they are used, you can relax and enjoy a leisurely meal because the fire symbols are obscured by the occupant.

The fire lines stimulate appetite and conversation for diners when entering a dining room but do not after one is seated—a perfect combination to induce suitable feelings for a dining experience.

The next chair combines fire and water elements. The horns' round oscillating shape ending with the triangular hooks combine water and fire. Visually sizzling, this piece commands attention in almost any setting, as does the person who decides to own this chair. Be sure to give the owner ample attention, for he or she will likely want to be the center of attention.

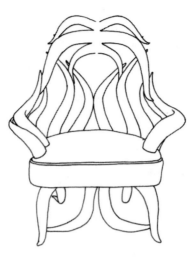

By choosing a chair with both fire and water, a person expresses the desire to be noticed.

Square, squat, and chunky chairs fully upholstered to the floor exhibit the quintessential line of earth. Appearing sturdy, these chairs are designed to be used for long periods of time, especially if they have an ottoman or footrest. How many there are in a space and how large they are will indicate whether the earth quality is on the positive side (stability) or challenged (stubbornness).

The more club-type chairs in a home, the more resistant to change a person might be.

A chair with a round or arched back carries the aura of the metal element. Although an arch is not a circle, which is the shape of metal, a round back moves the eye onward. Stimulating and yet formal, metal elements at once generate ideas and obligate one to adhere to social protocol. Metal refines but can constrain, and often those who have this elemental line in abundance are asserting their desire for appropriate behavior and manners.

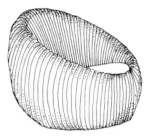

By choosing a chair with a metal element, a host is asking you to be attentive and to have acceptable manners.

Twisting and turning lines that oscillate freely while moving in all directions capture the spirit of agitated water. The degree of the turn is important to note. The tighter the line, the more frenzied is the image. The metal garden chair in the picture is at once fanciful and invigorating like a swim in a cold river. Almost asking you to feel like a guest at the Mad Hatter's tea party and be witty and brazen, this chair suggests you should not be laid back.

Fanciful and invigorating like a swim in a cold river, this Mad Hatter's tea party chair would be chosen by a person who likes to be surrounded by witty, fast-paced people.

The classroom's desk chair is the perfect example of the wood element. Straight-backed and leggy with no distracting embellishments, this chair communicates a seriousness of purpose. When comfort is minimized, alertness is safeguarded. Choosing austere-lined chairs with minimum comfort is communicating life's seriousness.

Straight lines express a tension that promotes alertness. A home filled with chairs that have mostly continuous, unbending lines expresses the wood elemental. Wood encourages one to change and discourages idleness.

A sparse, straight-backed chair is asking you to pay attention and be alert. Choosing this for a dining chair indicates a person who may not be as nurturing as others.

Because a person is likely to have more chairs than any other individual piece of furniture, discerning a common elemental thread can make uncovering a person's elemental persona easier. Because it is more likely that there will be many different elemental styles of chairs, observing what they are can usually confirm both the expressed and hidden elements of the one who chose them.

26

THE TABLE

I magine life without tables. We'd be crouching down to balance objects or have to tie them around our waist to keep them close by. Tables give us access to possessions. There is not a table in my house that is without art objects or useful materials. In fact, a table in my office has so much useful material on it that I have not seen it for years.

A table's size, shape, and base can disclose a great deal. I have been teaching nationwide in adult learning centers, and invariably the classrooms are filled with long, narrow tables. These tables are about two-thirds of the width of a classic folding table, and because of their diminutive width more students can be packed into a classroom. It has been observed that more learning takes place when a classroom's size is limited. Not so today; it is the size of the bottom line that motivates. Scope-ing these tables is easy: the desire to make money outweighs concern for human comfort or learning.

TABLE SIZE

Many times the more important the function, the larger the table. Moreover, a table's width determines how far away those sitting around it will be. Wide dining room tables discourage intimacy. I had a client who purchased a seventy-two-inch round dining table. This incredibly large circumference kept diners from communicating easily with those sitting across. As was the prevailing theme in this client's life, appearance was far more important than comfort or creating a forum for socializing.

On the other hand, years ago when I lived in the country my family of three dined daily around a classic ice cream table. We had a rustic lifestyle, and everyone was needed, from my son, who fed the chickens, to the adults, who split firewood to fuel a wood stove and tended the acre vegetable garden. We relied on each other for survival, and sitting at a table that had room for only plates brought us physically close in a world that relied on our working intimately together. Today, years later, living in Florida with all the conveniences of modern life, we dine on a conventionally sized table. Because we are not as dependent on each other for physical survival, a tiny round table feels unsuitable.

Tables in front of couches serve another purpose. Large coffee tables sitting in front of sofas provide ample surfaces on which to place objects, drinks, snacks, or sometimes feet. Selecting a commodious table for this area often indicates the desire to provide luxuries for enjoyment. The more spacious a surface, the more likely it is that human needs are paramount.

TABLE SHAPE

Feeling aligned to a shape indicates to some measure how we prefer to communicate. Notice if a person has a preference for one particular shape. If round is chosen for a gathering room, it indicates that this person likes ideas to flow and conversations to be ongoing. Yet the person may dine at a rectangular table, which suggests a desire for clearly defined family roles. Consider how shape influences activities.

What Choosing a Shape Might Mean

 Fire: Although not a shape for most tables, a fire shape can be defined by the position of chairs around a table. Choosing this configuration suggests desiring heated exchange of ideas or giving the person who is sitting solo authority or control.

If chairs are positioned to form a triangle, a person may want the exchange to be charged.

Square: Stability is desired.

 Round: Wants conversation to flow and good
manners to be displayed.

 Kidney shape: Wants people to feel relaxed and not
pressured.

Rectangle: Interesting, in-depth conversations
are preferred.

How far apart the chairs are around a dining room table indicates a person's willingness to become intimate. When we are seated within the distance where we can feel another person's body heat, we tend to want to feel relaxed and familiar with others. Diners tend to stay for a long time and converse with enthusiasm when placed in close proximity to each other. Placing people too far apart will extinguish an easy conversational flow and put up a shield separating those around a table.

Note how close or far the seating is around a dining table. The closer people are positioned, the more relaxed is the desired atmosphere.

Consider a head table or dais used for formal occasions. No table's position and shape so clearly defines the desire to separate and distinguish one set of guests from another. While these typically are the honored guests, they will not find sitting there conducive to conversation or intimacy.

TABLE BASES

Notice if pedestals or legs are preferred. Are the legs straight and plain or curved and ornate? The choice of leg style can disclose information as discussed in Part IV. In addition to knowing what the individual style bespeaks, it is telling to observe the base's stability. When a rickety table is not repaired, one can only imagine what other things are not attended to in lives.

One of the best cooks I know uses an old farm table with a deep apron on which to dine. It is a treat to be invited to dinner, for one can rightly expect a sumptuous meal. More than once, I have hurried to my seat, only to have my knees thump against the lower band of the table's apron. Moreover, her tall friends cannot push in their chair enough to make sitting at this table comfortable. The message is mixed. On one hand her time and talent are given to preparing food; on the other she provides a rather uncomfortable place to dine.

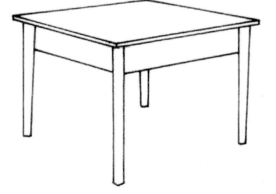

Choosing a table with a low apron communicates a mixed message, for care must be given not to hurt one's legs each time one sits down.

Tables are used communally more than any other piece of furniture, and their choice tells a great deal about the owner's attitude toward interacting.

27

THE BED

Like underwear, a bed often reveals dimensions not normally exposed. I remember being stunned when one of my mother's high school friends visited us and hung her black undergarments to dry in my bathroom. Black was, in my mind, only for exotic ladies, not my mothers' friends!

A bedroom is a space where people should feel free to express themselves totally. What is displayed often has special meaning. A favored sculpture, a treasured family photograph, and a few personal belongings resting by the side of a bed can tell you what is important. The focal point of a bedroom is, of course, the bed, that single piece of furniture that has the responsibility to comfort us physically and emotionally.

The celebrity status of Yoko Ono and John Lennon gave them the liberty to blend personal and business life. Much of their daily business was conducted from bed. Photographs give us a peek at what for many is the ultimate lifestyle: the opportunity to combine work with leisure and pleasure.

There is something seductive about being able to conduct life's everyday functions from bed; however, for us more ordinary folks such behavior is rather disturbing. One of my clients, a young divorced woman, made it crystal clear that her favorite place at home was in bed. She ate, worked, and socialized with her friends and son while in bed. It came as no surprise to discover that she felt melancholy most of the time and was hard-pressed to feel optimistic. Her relationship with her son was strained, and she extracted little joy from life. A bed, like dessert at the end of a meal, is something to be enjoyed at the end of a day.

Further, this client's bedroom was the only room in her home that was completely finished. Sponged, light blue walls set off her king-size bed, which was covered in various shades of blue, with an abundance of pillows that a sultan could envy. Her favorite piece of furniture, a heavy antique chest from Sweden, stood against the entrance wall, buffering her from the rest of the household. A solitary nightstand projected a message that she was not ready for another relationship, and the absence of any chair gave her eleven-year-old son the choice of either sitting on her bed or not at all. What is not present is as important as what is.

> **Those who conduct too many activities from bed may be withdrawing from full participation in and responsibilities of life.**

All headboards should be scoped by their shape and the material. For example, a brass headboard with undulating lines has both the metal and water elements. The following will reveal what common headboard designs can signify.

FOUR-POSTER BED

A four-poster bed creates a room within a room. A canopy stretching across the top precisely renders the edges, separating a bed from the rest of the room. The feel of a canopied four-poster bed is not unlike the bedsheet tent many of us fashioned as children to feel protected and sheltered. It exudes safety and imbues those in it with importance. The person who chooses to sleep in a canopied four-poster bed likes the feeling of being safely enshrined.

A bed with a footboard restricts movement and is not currently in vogue in our society, which esteems personal freedom. However, when selected, it is a signal that a person may want and need additional support or control. I once knew a woman who purchased a rare, antique four-poster bed that had both a headboard and a footboard. Her executive husband loved to collect rare antiques, so his conundrum was whether to praise her for this find or feel annoyed that he had to squeeze his six-foot-six frame into a confined space. Was this purchase a way of subtly controlling him? She probably knew that his delight with the collectible would overshadow his daily discomfort.

When a four-poster bed has fabric stretched across the top, the four uprights cease replicating a fire shape and change a bed's appearance to earth or wood, depending on what size the bed's mattress is. King-size beds are earth shaped, and queen-size beds are wood.

Swagging fabric over the horizontal supports transposes the straight wood line to an undulating water one. Moreover, it transforms a formal look to one more casual. More aligned with the water element, those who drape a four-poster bed are expressing a playfulness and willingness to go with the flow.

THE SOLID HEADBOARD

A solid unbroken headboard provides a contiguous surface on which to rest. Even if the headboard is detailed with bas-relief, drawings, or carvings, the overall shape takes precedence over the details. Thus a solid headboard is judged by the perimeter shape.

Rectangular headboards are favored by those who like to take charge and risk beginning new projects. Typically these persons do not like to linger in bed and have fast-paced lives. They are averse to being diverted from their chosen path and abhor distractions.

A rectangular headboard suggests a person who does not need a great deal of time to make a decision.

A round or oval headboard suggests inventiveness and intrigue and is often chosen by those who like to spend time going over future plans. It is not unusual to find one who chooses this shape conducting business from bed.

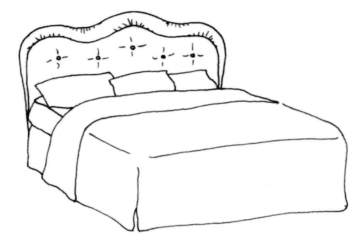

*Round or oval headboards are often selected by those who like to
go over plans carefully and thoroughly.*

Upholstered Headboard

With a voluminous pliant surface, upholstered headboards can be
the ultimate in comfort. Although the fabric and color may express
another element, comfort is a by-product of the water element. An
upholstered headboard gives way to a body in the same way water
does. This kind of headboard needs regular care and replacement
more frequently than one composed of another material. A person
who would choose to attend to home furnishings is, to some degree,
a caretaker. When selecting an object with planned obsolescence,
one is communicating acceptance of life cycles.

Headboard as Entertainment Center

Finally, when a headboard includes an entire entertainment system,
the earth element is expressed. The more needs serviced, the more
earthlike it is. Years ago I read that Barbra Streisand not only had
an entire stereo system as part of her headboard but also a refrigerator and cabinets holding dishes and glasses. It seemed at once
exotic and cozy to be able to satisfy one's every whim while in bed.
The more items found surrounding a bed, the more one needs to
feel secure.

A person who needs security will opt to have an entire entertainment center for a headboard.

No Headboard

Those who choose no supportive ornamentation at the head of a bed are settling for less comfort. A simple sleeping platform is the ultimate in utilitarian. There is no lingering, lounging, or spending extraneous time in a bed without supports to lean against. Not likely to be forgiving, one who chooses to ignore this piece of furniture may be a taskmaster.

Those who give no thought or care to making their bed inviting are denying themselves a place on which to spin their dreams. Beds have an esteemed place historically. Births and deaths are major life cycles for which a bed is often used. In India's Mutabani region, which abuts the Himalayan Mountains, the families reserve a special room with nothing but an elaborate bed that is occupied only by the bride and groom during the first two weeks of their marriage.

Those who wish to be absolved from responsibility, who try to be insulated from any unpleasantness, will tend to overdecorate a bed's surface. Just as too much protective clothing in winter makes us inflexible, too many pillows, coverlets, toys, stuffed animals, flounces, and drapes on a bed render its occupants stagnant in mind, body, and spirit.

A bed in some ways is like a good mother—there to comfort but not be relied on too often.

28

SHIFTING INTO BALANCE

I was traveling alone in my favorite part of our country when I was offered an ice-cold glass of water. A young man serving me urged me to replenish the fluid that is sucked out by the brutal dryness of the high New Mexico desert. While I sipped this delicious liquid, he shared this story. He had dreamed of this spot even before he had any knowledge of its existence. The difference between one state of being and another, he suggested, was only the form chosen. Illustrating his point of view, he recounted this Native American tale.

A young boy sitting at the feet of his wise old grandfather observed a bird and asked, "Grandfather, why can't I fly?"

"What makes you think you cannot?" his grandfather said while gazing up at the sky. "The creatures who fly believe they can."

"Well, then," said the boy, "if that is so, I will fling myself off the mesa and fly."

"That is not possible, my son," said the old man, whose face was as lined as mud baked by the summer sun.

"But, grandfather, you just told me that if I wanted to I could!"

"No, my son, I said you have to believe, and belief is like the calluses on the hands of one who works the soil. The results of belief come only after hard work."

And so the young boy worked at flying for most of his life in the only way he knew how. During nighttime dreams or reveries of daydreaming, he pictured himself flying. In his dreams he soared over the mountains, sat on the highest pine trees, and flew above the routes of passageways carved by water across the plain.

Finally he too was a grandfather, and one day his grandson asked him the same question he had asked his grandfather those many years ago. The answered he offered was the same one he had been told. Over time he, like his grandfather, had realized that flying is the same as any dream, and it comes to pass only when we shift the form of the dream to meet our reality. Now he too knew that nothing is impossible, only the desire to experience it in one way. And so his grandson also learned to fly, in his way.

We must not be limited by expectations, because relationships must be dealt with in the present with what exists. We can walk on water, through walls, and on a cloud so long as we make a path to follow that is not limited by expectations. If we care to fly, we shall.

AFTERWORD

For all of you trying to find the sometimes elusive sense of contentment, I urge you not to think of it as too amorphous to grasp or out of reach. Contentment is present in each moment. Only our perception needs adjusting.

You alone can harvest a fulfilling life. Finding a compatible partner is a bonus, like a scrumptious dessert—lovely but not necessary for a nourishing diet. And so, dear readers, I leave you hopefully with the knowledge of how to choose someone with whom you will thrive. Until that someone should chance into your life, know that you are enough.

Be empty of permanence
But full of life
Set a course to fulfill a purpose which needs no form
Yet shape it, to hold in the mind's eye
See all things and yet be not blinded by
Trying to be all things

Be untroubled with what's on your plate
Be comfortable with the gifts already bestowed
And what you have chosen as your purpose

We are no less nor more than moments toward actualization
What we choose to believe becomes our story
Do not accept another's dream
Even when yours is hidden from view

Dream not too myopically or too grand
The essence of life is in each moment
Look and leap not
You are enough, here and now

Nancilee Wydra, 1998

BIBLIOGRAPHY

Ackerman, Diane. *A Natural History of the Senses*. New York: Random House, 1990.

Beinfield, Harriet, and Korngold, Efrem. *Between Heaven and Earth: A Guide to Chinese Medicine*. New York: Ballantine Books, 1991.

Birren, Faber. *Color & Human Response*. New York: Van Nostrand Reinhold, 1978.

Blakeslee, Thomas R. *Beyond the Conscious Mind*. New York: Plenum Press, 1996.

Boger, Louise Ad. *The Complete Guide to Furniture Styles*. New York: Charles Scribner's Sons, 1969.

Caesar, Sid. *Where Have I Been: An Autobiography*. New York: Crown Publishers, 1982.

Campbell, Joseph. *Power of Myth*. New York: Doubleday, 1988.

Gallagher, Winifred. *The Power of Place*. New York: Harper Perennial, 1993.

Gallagher, Winifred. *Just the Way You Are*. New York: Random House, 1996.

Goleman, Daniel. *Emotional Intelligence*. New York: Bantam Books, 1994.

Hall, Edward T. *The Silent Language*. New York: Anchor Books, Doubleday, 1959.

Hall, Edward T. *The Hidden Dimension*. New York: Anchor Books, Doubleday, 1966.

Heelas, Paul, and Lock, Andrew. *Indigenous Psychologies: The Anthropology of the Self.* New York: Academic Press, 1981.

Liberman, Jacob. *Light Medicine of the Future.* Santa Fe: Bear & Company, Inc., 1991.

Marcus, Claire Cooper. *House as a Mirror of Self.* Berkeley, CA: Conari Press, 1995.

Massey Anne. *Interior Designing of the 20th Century.* London: Thames and Hudson Ltd., 1990.

Petraglia, Patricia P. *Sotheby's Guide to American Furniture.* New York: Simon & Shuster, 1995.

Pinker, Steven. *How the Mind Works.* New York: W. W. Norton & Company, 1997.

Vroon, Piet. *Smell: The Secret Seducer.* New York: Farrar, Straus and Giroux, 1994.

Wydra, Nancilee. *Designing Your Happiness: A Contemporary Look at Feng Shui.* Torrance, CA: Heian International, 1995.

Wydra, Nancilee. *Feng Shui: The Book of Cures.* Chicago: Contemporary Books, 1996.

Wydra, Nancilee. *Feng Shui in the Garden.* Chicago: Contemporary Books, 1997.

Zukav, Gary. *The Dancing Wu Li Masters.* New York: William Morrow and Company, Inc., 1979.

INDEX

275

ABOUT THE AUTHOR

Nancilee Wydra, author of three other books on feng shui, has been studying the effects of place on people for more than twenty-five years. Founder of the Feng Shui Institute of America, she trains, lectures, and consults nationwide. She lives in Vero Beach, Florida.

The author invites you to set up study groups and notify her about this by mail. You will be notified when she is visiting your town. For this and other information about feng shui training, general classes, or lectures, contact:

Nancilee Wydra
Feng Shui Institute of America
P.O. Box 488
Wabasso, FL 32970
1-888-488-FSIA
fax: (561) 589-1611
E-mail: Windwater8@aol.com
Internet site: www.windwater.com